End Times in Easy Terms

End Times
In Easy Terms

Individual or small group study on the end times in easy to understand terms

End Times

In Easy Terms

Dan W. Ingram, Th.M

End Times in Easy Terms

For questions, comments or suggestions for another book please write to:
Dan Ingram c/o
Sunrise Baptist Church
12115 Shaw Road East
Puyallup, Wa. 98374
Or email: revdan@sunrisebaptist.org

Unless otherwise noted, Scripture taken from the HOLY BIBLE, NEW INTERNATIONAL VERSION®. Copyright © 1973, 1978, 1984 International Bible Society. Used by permission of Zondervan. All rights reserved.

End Times in Easy Terms

Dedication

To all those who encouraged me through the years; I will never forget those at my home church in which I grew up at Berry Street Baptist Church in Springdale, Arkansas who had such a great impact on my early Christian thought. To the many people in the churches with which I've been privileged to share ministry over the years. To my parents, grandparents and especially my wife Lorrie and my children; Alicia, Rebecca, Isaac and Hannah, who are wonderful workers in the ministry. Thanks to Sunrise Baptist in Puyallup, Washington for allowing me to lead you in expressing our true devotion and Kingdom living to Jesus. I applaud and thank everyone God has put in my life to make my teaching ministry possible. Thanks to my wife Lorrie, friend Kenny Poague and my father-in-law Harold for their help in editing.

To God be the glory!

-- Dan

End Times in Easy Terms

Contents

Chapter 1: Introduction Pg. 7

Chapter 2: Are we living in the last days? Pg. 17

Chapter 3: The next great event in prophecy: the Rapture Pg. 25

Chapter 4: The Big Question: When is Jesus coming back? Pg.33

Chapter 5: What will happen at the Rapture? Pg. 47

Chapter 6: What will our bodies be like in heaven? Pg.59

Chapter 7: A Brief Look at the Tribulation Pg. 77

Chapter 8: What is God's message through the Great Tribulation? Pg. 109

Chapter 9: The Millennium Pg. 119

Chapter 10: What will heaven be like? Pg. 131

Chapter 11: What happens after the end of Revelation? Pg. 141

Chapter 12: Kid's Ask Pg. 145

Chapter 13: Conclusion Pg. 151

Appendix A: How to be ready. Pg. 153

Appendix B: Date setters through history. Pg. 156

> *"Confusion is a word we have invented for an order which is not yet understood"*
> — Henry Miller

Chapter 1

Are You Confused Too?

THUNDER CRASHED! It was so loud and immediate that it literally startled me out of my office chair in my little country church. Violent thunderstorms are not that unusual in Arkansas but that thunder clap was different for me. When I heard it, I almost immediately sensed God telling me something.

Now, I'm not one of those guys that always says, "God told me this…" or "God told me that…" and to be honest, I rarely say that. I do however sense that at times God tries to get our attention and point out specifics of the scripture through circumstances. The day the thunder sounded was one of those days for me.

Right after the thunder clap I sensed the Lord saying, "*My judgment is coming just like that; swiftly, quickly and with*

End Times in Easy Terms

authority." After I sensed that, I was a little shaken and I wondered if it was just "me" after the scare of the thunder. So I said, "Lord, if that was You speaking to me, please confirm that and show me in Your Word." The next thing I did I would not necessarily advise, especially in trying to get a word from the Lord, but I did it. I closed my eyes, opened my Bible, and blindly put my finger on a verse. I then opened my eyes and read the verse where my finger landed. I was pointing to Isaiah 29:6, "The LORD Almighty will come with thunder and earthquake and great noise, with windstorm and tempest and flames of a devouring fire."

OK, now I was more than a little nervous. The word "thunder" is only mentioned two times in Isaiah in the New International Version and only once in the King James and here I was pointing to it! So what does it mean?

I've pondered many times the meaning of that two to three minute meeting with God, and I've come to the conclusion that I'm not sure what it meant except that (1) God didn't reveal to me anything new. He just brought to my attention something that He already said. (2) God still points things out to us. (3) God shows us and confirms to us what He is up to through His Word. (4) Judgment is coming.

I tell the "thunder story" because God does confirm things to us from His Word when we seek Him. When we are

End Times in Easy Terms

confused, especially about the topic of the end times, His Word is the only place to go for understanding and comfort.

Let me introduce myself and let you in on a little history of how this book came to be. Let's go back in time a moment. I became a Christian when I was eight and I remember as a youngster, a traveling evangelist coming to our church and he introduced me to a new term. He told us that the study of the end times is called *eschatology (es-ka-tol'-ogy)*. This preacher spoke a whole week, every night, on the book of Revelation. He was so animated and seemed to make the book of Revelation come alive!

Every night at that church in Arkansas, USA, I would sit on the third row, by myself and take careful notes. Those were days before CD's, DVD's, and MP3's so my parents bought his record for me and I listened to it constantly over and over for almost a year. I studied it so much that I was convinced that I had the whole Revelation thing figured out.

I have been a pastor for many years now and many times in college and in my personal studies, I have studied the book of Revelation and other prophetic books of the Bible. During those studies I found that I certainly was not alone in my confusion. I read several books by other authors and many of them did not agree on "the when" and "the how" these end time events will happen.

I remember studying Revelation in my first year in Bible College when I asked a professor about a particular topic on the

End Times in Easy Terms

end times. I was reading a commentary with which I did not agree and I said to the professor, "Do you think someone is dumb enough to still believe in this particular idea?" And I'll never forget his response; he said, "Well, that's what I believe in personally!" I felt embarrassed and was sorry about what I said out of my confusion and ignorance.

Over the years, in my experience, I've come to the conclusion that there are good solid conservative believers who agree how everything is going to end, but who might disagree on the details of how they are going to happen. We agree that the thunderous judgment is coming, but the when and the how are still debated.

In considering that most people have neither the books nor the time or knowledge in the Bible languages, and because my children were asking many questions about the rapture and tribulation, I was prompted to write a more simplified book about the many questions that people have concerning the end times.

I decided to write on this subject when my son Isaac, eleven years old at the time, kept asking questions and wanting a visual outline of the end times. Like many other Christians he was interested in what was going to happen and wanted to know more.

As I searched my personal library and Christian bookstores and catalogs, I discovered I could not find a book written to my satisfaction on a simpler level to either young

End Times in Easy Terms

Christians or Christians who just want a general easier to understand Biblical guideline of some of the events that will take place in what the Bible calls the end times. This book is the answer to my search.

As you read you will notice that I have not added any alternative interpretations of the topics I address except for a few in the chapter on the tribulation and millennium. There are many viewpoints, interpretations, and thoughts on the last times and the order in which to put them. I will tell you up front that this is not a scholarly book. If you are part of a denominational affiliation you will probably see the end times through a particular theological lens. This is not a book on how to interpret the last times; there are a lot of books about that topic if you wish further study. I am simply giving a straight forward conservative viewpoint with plenty of scripture.

I will be teaching from the standpoint of the Pre-Tribulation Rapture and a Pre-Millennial interpretation, both of which we will discuss in a later chapter.

Please note that the viewpoints set forth in this book are not taught as the way the end times will be as set in stone. There is a lot of room for discussion. There will be many topics and discussions not addressed in a more simplified book such as this one.

As always, I encourage every believer to be like the believers in Acts 17:11 "Now the Bereans were of more noble character than the Thessalonians, for they received the message with great eagerness and examined the Scriptures every day to see if what Paul said was true." I always encourage every believer to read the scriptures, pray and make up their own mind and not just follow one book, church or denominational teaching. Search the scriptures daily!

I have noticed that children ask some of the best questions, even the questions that adults will not ask. For this reason I have included a section called "Kids Ask" along with a list of study questions for personal devotional study or for use in a small group setting. Consider your answers to these questions carefully. These questions are not only given to help you learn but also as insightful thought questions for your life or the individuals in your group.

This study could take off in many different directions with many topics and areas that would be interesting and fun to study, but due to the nature of this book towards simplicity, those topics will have to be explored by the reader in their own time.

So, are you confused too? It is my prayer that as you read and study through this book that, just as I searched God's Word for confirmation in the meaning of the thunder, the Bible will speak to you concerning the meaning of these end time events. The Bible comes alive when we look at the scriptures in context and when we read and believe them for what they say to us as God speaks to us through His word.

End Times in Easy Terms

Study Questions

1. What made you decide to study this book or be a part of this small group? _____

_____

2. Before you get into this study, what are your initial thoughts or ideas about what the "last days" are?

_____

_____

_____

3. How were you brought up as a child to believe in "prophecy" or "God's wrath or judgment"?

_____

_____

_____

4. What do you think about the author's "method" at the moment of blindly opening the Bible and pointing to a Bible verse? Have you ever done that?

_____

_____

_____

End Times in Easy Terms

5. Have you ever studied about the end times before? Why now?

_____

_____

_____

End Times in Easy Terms

> How beautiful the leaves grow old. How full of light and color are their last days.
>
> John Burroughs

Chapter 2

Are We Living In The Last Days?

As pastor, two of the most popular questions asked of me are; "Do you think we're living in the end times?" and "Do you really think the coming of the Lord is near?" I think I can definitely answer the first question, but as to the other questions I'm only going to have to look at scripture and let the Bible answer those.

I personally believe we are living in the end times or as the Bible calls it "the last days." To answer this question we must first examine how the Bible defines these terms.

End Times in Easy Terms

What is meant by the term "last days?" The best place to find that answer is IN THE BIBLE! The first reference to this term in the New Testament is found in Acts 2:17, "'In the last days, God says, I will pour out my Spirit on all people. Your sons and daughters will prophesy, your young men will see visions and your old men will dream dreams."

Acts 2:17 is a quotation from the Old Testament book of Joel 2:28-32. The prophet Joel said this about 650 years before Jesus was born, to describe a special time the New Testament calls the "last days". So what is the "last days"?

The New Commentary on the Whole Bible: New Testament describes the last days in Acts 2:17 this way, "This phrase is used in the New Testament to designate the entire New Testament period which precedes the Parousia of Christ."

Say what? Those are some BIG words! Let's break it down. The term "Parousia" pronounced (pa-ru-si-ah) is a Greek word that simply means "presence" or "arriving." In this case, "last times" means the life that we are living now on earth that will take us right up to the arrival or coming of Jesus at the rapture. The rapture is the future event of Jesus' coming and taking away all the Christians at once. We will talk about the rapture and tribulation in later chapters.

2 Timothy 3:1-5 tells us, "But mark this: There will be terrible times in the last days. People will be lovers of themselves, lovers of money, boastful, proud, abusive, disobedient to their

parents, ungrateful, unholy, without love, unforgiving, slanderous, without self-control, brutal, not lovers of the good, treacherous, rash, conceited, lovers of pleasure rather than lovers of God—having a form of godliness but denying its power. Have nothing to do with them."

Paul says that the last days will be terrible times. Describing what the people will be like, he warns Timothy to have nothing to do with them. Paul understood that he was living in the last days, the days before Jesus comes again.

The writer of Hebrews 1:1-2 said that God has spoken to us in these last days, "In the past God spoke to our forefathers through the prophets at many times and in various ways, but in these last days he has spoken to us by his Son, whom he appointed heir of all things, and through whom he made the universe." The writer understood that the people of his time were living in the last days or the days before the return of Jesus.

The Apostle James gives a rebuke to the rich people for hording wealth in the last days, in James 5:3 he says "Your gold and silver are corroded. Their corrosion will testify against you and eat your flesh like fire. You have hoarded wealth in the last days." James understood that he was living in the days before the return of Christ.

Peter tells believers that scoffers and mockers will come in the last days and make fun of the coming (Parousia) of Christ. 2 Peter 3:3-4, reminds us "First of all, you must understand that in the last days scoffers will come, scoffing and following their own evil desires. They will say, "Where is this 'coming' he promised? Ever since our fathers died, everything goes on as it has since the beginning of creation." Peter understood that he was living in the last days.

We clearly see that in the New Testament the term "last days" refers to the time we are living in now before the return of Jesus at the rapture. All of the New Testament writers understood that they were living in the last days. We do not know *when* the rapture will happen but we do know we are living in the time before it has happened.

We also know that we are more than 2000 years closer to the rapture than when the New Testament writers wrote their letters, but the coming of Jesus still has not happened. The "last days" have been going on for over the last 2000 years.

The age we are living in right now is, I believe, a special time. Remember that the last days mark the time before Jesus returns. Because we do not know *when* Jesus will return, we have an urgency to be ready. The urgency will be explained in a later chapter.

It's been a long time since the Bible was written. How then can the last days go on for so long? 2 Peter 3:8 says "But do not forget this one thing, dear friends: With the Lord a day is like a thousand years, and a thousand years are like a day." So even though it's been over 2000 years, we are still living in the same

End Times in Easy Terms

last days as the Apostles. What this means is that the Lord does not count time as we do. As we live in these last days, we cannot become impatient for the Lord to come to take us to heaven.

As believers, the fact that we ARE living in the last days should excite us because it means that every day is one day closer to Jesus' coming and Christians going to heaven where there are no more tears, pain or sorrow. Everything will be wonderful and perfect (Revelation 21).

But you don't want to go to heaven QUITE YET? You still want to experience some wonderful things here on this earth like marriage or children or other things you have not experienced yet? That's ok! There are some things I would like to see before I go to heaven too. All I can say about this is that it is up to God. We need to live life for God the very best we can every day, staying close to Jesus through His Word. If Jesus does not come back soon and we have time to experience those things we want, then we should consider those as blessings from God.

As long as God allows us to be here, living in His kingdom, we also have opportunity everyday to show people the love of God. Every day we are here, we have opportunity to love God, love others and live the life God calls us to live.

However if Jesus comes back soon and you go to heaven, it will be so wonderful that you will not even know what you missed here on this earth. Revelation 21:4-5 says, "He will wipe every tear from their eyes. There will be no more death or mourning or crying or pain, for the old order of things has passed away." He who was seated on the throne said, "I am making everything new!" Then he said, "Write this down, for these words are trustworthy and true."

The important question is "are you ready if Jesus should return today?" If you would like to know more about what it takes to be ready, please look at the section in the back of the book called "HOW TO BE READY." See Appendix A.

Study Questions:

1. What is the Greek word that means the "presence" or "arriving" of Christ?

_____

2. What does the term "last days" refer to in the New Testament?

_____
_____

3. About how long have we been in the "last days?"

_____
_____

End Times in Easy Terms

4. Are you ready to go if Jesus Christ arrived right now? Why or why not? _____

_____

_____

5. In your opinion what is the most exciting thing about living in the last days?

_____

_____

_____

_____

6. What is the scariest part for you as you think about living in the last days?

_____

_____

_____

_____

> *Nowhere is salvation conceived of as a flight from history as in Greek thought; it is always the coming of God to man in history. Man does not ascend to God; God descends to man.*
>
> George Eldon Ladd

CHAPTER 3

The Next Great Event in Prophecy: The Rapture

The coming of Jesus for His church is called the RAPTURE. The particular word "rapture" is never mentioned in scripture. It comes from a Latin word "rapare" pronounced (ra-pare). In the Greek, when the "rapture" is talked about, the word is "harpazo" which means "to snatch away or to take out." So the rapture means that the church (all believers in Jesus) will be taken out of the earth and up to heaven when Jesus comes again. Those who are not believers will be left to go through the tribulation.

End Times in Easy Terms

WHY IS THE RAPTURE SOMETHING WE NEED TO KNOW ABOUT?

The rapture is important because:

1) The Bible speaks of it so much:

2) Knowing about it gives us comfort: Isaiah 40:1 & 10: "Comfort, comfort my people, says your God. Lift up your voice with a shout, lift it up, do not be afraid; say to the towns of Judah, "Here is your God!" See, the Sovereign LORD comes with power, and His arm rules for Him. See, His reward is with Him, and His recompense accompanies Him"

Sometimes we get tired and we just want to say, "come quickly Lord Jesus!" We know the coming of the Lord will put an end to all heartache and troubles we experience here on earth and that brings us comfort.

Paul says the knowledge of Jesus' coming gives us hope as Christians in Titus 2:13, "we wait for the blessed hope—the glorious appearing of our great God and Savior, Jesus Christ." That is comfort. 2 Peter 3:12, says "look forward to the day of God and speed its coming." That gives us comfort. Paul in 1 Thessalonians 4:18 speaking of the rapture says, "Comfort one another with these words." Even the very last prayer and statement of the Bible in Revelation 22:20 "Even so come Lord Jesus." That gives us COMFORT!

3) It spurs us on to live holy lives: Realizing that the Lord Jesus Himself may appear at any time encourages us to live

holy lives. 2 Peter 3:11 tells us, "You ought to live holy and godly lives as you look forward to the day of God." The Bible says in 1 John 2:28 "And now, dear children, continue in him, so that when he appears we may be confident and unashamed before him at his coming."

Again in Luke 12:35-37 we are told to ""Be dressed for service and well prepared, as though you were waiting for your master to return from the wedding feast. Then you will be ready to open the door and let him in the moment he arrives and knocks. There will be special favor for those who are ready and waiting for his return."

The rapture, the next great event in history, is looming in our future. What kind of Christian you would be if this fact did not spur you on to good works, to stay faithful to the Lord? The rapture of the church is vitally important to our future as well as our present!

The Rapture is a wonderful promise we are given over and over in scripture. The promise of the return of Jesus is for those who believe in Him. Look at the following scriptures and just think about the great promise that Jesus gave us when He said that HE IS coming back again someday.

End Times in Easy Terms

PROMISE VERSES OF JESUS' RETURN

1 Corinthians 11:26 "For whenever you eat this bread and drink this cup, you proclaim the Lord's death until he comes."

1 Thessalonians 2:19 "For what is our hope, our joy, or the crown in which we will glory in the presence of our Lord Jesus when he comes? Is it not you?"

Hebrews 9:28 "So Christ was sacrificed once to take away the sins of many people; and he will appear a second time, not to bear sin, but to bring salvation to those who are waiting for him."

Titus 2:13 "wait for the blessed hope—the glorious appearing of our great God and Savior, Jesus Christ."

Matthew 25:31 "When the Son of Man comes in his glory, and all the angels with him, he will sit on his throne in heavenly glory."

Acts 1:11 "The men of Galilee said," "why do you stand here looking into the sky? This same Jesus, who has been taken from you into heaven, will come back in the same way you have seen him go into heaven."

WOW! I think Jesus is trying to tell us that we need to be ready because He IS coming back again.

WHAT ABOUT PEOPLE WHO DISBELIEVE AND LAUGH AT THE RAPTURE?

Even though we KNOW Jesus is coming back, there are people who laugh and make fun of not only the Rapture but also those of us who believe it. That is OK because the Bible has already told us that people will laugh at us. Listen to 2 Peter 3:3-4, "First of all, you must understand that in the last days scoffers (*mockers*) will come, scoffing and following their own evil desires. They will say, "Where is this 'coming' he promised? Ever since our fathers died, everything goes on as it has since the beginning of creation."

People like this have always been around and will always be around until Jesus comes back. As Christians we have to stand strong in the faith and live for Christ!

Study Questions

1. The word "rapture" is never mentioned in the Bible. Where do we get that word and why do we use it?

_____
_____

2. Even though we may not be able to fully understand the rapture or even agree on the details of it, why is it, in your opinion important to at least know about what the Bible says about the rapture?

_____
_____
_____

3. Even though the rapture might bring some comfort, do you think it might cause different emotions in others for different reasons? Why or why not?

_____
_____
_____
_____

End Times in Easy Terms

4. What verse or verses given in this chapter spoke to you the most about the rapture?

_____

_____

5. Even early on in the beginnings of the New Testament Church there were people who laughed and scoffed at the idea of a return of a "GOD" in the air. Have you ever felt this way or do you know people who feel this way about this topic?

_____

_____

6. What should be our Christian reaction to scoffers of God, the Bible or prophecy?

_____

_____

_____

> *Precisely because we cannot predict the moment, we must be ready at all moments.*
> — C.S. Lewis

Chapter 4

The Big Question: WHEN IS JESUS COMING BACK?

This is "THE" question that has been asked since Jesus went back to heaven over 2000 years ago. In fact Jesus' own disciples asked Him about it. In Mark 13:31-33, Jesus said about His coming "No one knows about that day or hour, not even the angels in heaven, nor the Son, but only the

Father. Be on guard! Be alert! You do not know when that time will come."

We know that He IS coming back, but the Bible says that we will not know when. That is why we must be ready.

FALSE DATE SETTERS HAVE BEEN AROUND FOR A LONG TIME

It is interesting that in my research I have found 100's of predictions setting the date of Christ's return over the years. It started very early when the Apostle Paul had to write to the church at Thessalonica to tell them of a rumor that the return of Christ had already happened! This is the very reason Paul wrote 1 Thessalonians 4-5, rumors were starting that early in history.

All through history in every generation and century there have been individuals and groups of people who have set specific dates and tried to predict the coming of Jesus. Over the years I have gathered several examples.

In a 124 page booklet put out in 1988 called, 88 Reasons Why the Rapture Could be in 1988, under the summary it says, "You only need one good solid reason why 1988 will be the church's Rapture. Here are 88 reasons why 1988 looks like the year of the church's Rapture for you to pick one from." Well, I hate to break the news but the Rapture DID NOT happen in 1988 as predicted by the author.

End Times in Easy Terms

In 1989 the same author put out another 85 page booklet called <u>The Final Shout Rapture Report 1989.</u> In this booklet he explains on page 1 of chapter 1, "Jesus is really coming and I believe it's this year! My mistake was that my mathematical calculations were off by one year." In the opening *Note from the Publisher* on page *iii* it says, "Jesus is coming and I would give it at least a 50% chance in 1989; if not then, an abundance of Scriptures point to 1992. However, if the birth dates of Christ are off one or two years, then it could be in 1990 or 1991. There seems to be a lot more evidence for '89 and '92 than any other time for the Rapture."

I have another 99 page booklet put out by Mission for the Coming Days called <u>Are You Ready for the Rapture? October 28, 1992.</u> On page 46 it says, "One must not try to set dates for the return of Christ with man's wisdom and knowledge. Some prophetic scholars of the past have missed possibly because of misinterpreting and miscalculating certain scriptures. But if God reveals the date, we can know for sure." On page 73 it goes on to state, "God gave the righteous more insight as the Rapture date drew nearer. God revealed the general time, the year 1992 first. Later, as judgment drew nearer, He revealed the month, October of 1992. Then, He revealed the date, 28th October. Next, the exact time, 24:000 of 28 October 1992 was revealed to us." The book gives us a warning on page 85, "God is the source who supplied this date to us. It might be wise to have second thoughts

End Times in Easy Terms

before you oppose it because you might be speaking against the Holy Spirit, if this is a revelation by God."

Again, I hate to break the news, but Jesus did not come back in October 1992 and I guess we know now that was not a revelation by God. I have included these illustrations for this reason; there are still dates that are set in the future about the coming of Jesus and the end of the world and this age. The Mayan/Aztec calendars predict the end of the world on December 21, 2012, and even Sir Isaac Newton who discovered the laws of gravity and died in 1727 noted on a piece of paper that he believed the world would end in 2060.

I would like to remind us all that JESUS Himself said in Mark 13:32-33, "No one knows about that day or hour, not even the angels in heaven, nor the Son, but only the Father. Be on guard! Be alert! You do not know when that time will come." If Jesus said it, then that's good enough for me.

(PLEASE LOOK AT THE DATE SETTERS THROUGH HISTORY FOUND IN APPENDIX B)

The Bible lays out some guidelines for us to remember when we study about the return of Jesus at the rapture. God knew that in our sinfulness we would be confused about this issue. If we simply look at the Bible and examine what it says we have some principles that help us to understand this prophetic event.

End Times in Easy Terms

THE TIME IS UNINTENDED FOR US TO KNOW:

The disciples were asking about the end times and in Acts 1:7 it says "The Father sets those dates and they are not for you to know." When someone else sets a date, just smile, trust God and continue to live for God today, knowing that no one knows the day or hour.

IT WILL BE AT AN UNEXPECTED TIME:

Matthew 24:44, "be ready all the time. For the Son of Man will come when least expected." Notice that we are always commanded to look, watch, be ready and live like Jesus is coming today. If that is the case then the rapture has to be an IMMINENT event that means it could happen at any time or moment.

IT WILL BE BUSINESS AS USUAL WHEN JESUS COMES:

Life before the rapture will be normal. Just like the days before the flood happened, life went on as normal. Noah gave the warning but no one listened. Luke 17:26, "In those days before the flood, the people enjoyed banquets and parties and weddings right up to the time Noah entered his boat and the flood came to destroy them all."

The Bible tells us in Matthew 24:40-41 "Then shall two be in the field; the one shall be taken, and the other left. Two women shall be grinding at the mill; the one shall be taken, and the other left. I tell you, on that night two people will be sleeping in one bed; one will be taken and the other will be left." These verses clearly tell us that people will be working, sleeping and going about daily chores. It will be business as usual, and then the rapture will happen.

These verses in Luke and Matthew tell us that God will not blow the trumpet to get us prepared. He has already told us to be prepared. The next time the heavenly trumpet blows we are out of here! All preparation must be done now.

IT WILL BE AN UNPRECEDENTED TIME:

God has this time appointed. Jesus said that only God knows the day and hour. What if that hour is 2:48 tomorrow morning while you're in bed? Will you wake up alone? It's an unprecedented time that's already been appointed! Are you ready? No one knows the day or hour but when God's clock rings, what will happen to you?

CAN WE KNOW IF IT IS GETTING CLOSE?

Yes, Jesus gives us some clues to look for. Although we have just discovered that Jesus tells us that nobody knows WHEN He is coming back, He does give us some hints about what to look for as the time gets closer.

The hints that Jesus gives us are called signs. As you are traveling down a road, signs tell you important information you need as a driver. It's the same way in the Bible. The scripture tells us how to live our everyday lives and what to look for as the coming of Jesus gets closer every day.

There were some men in Jesus' day that tried to trap Him and make Him say wrong things either against the scripture or against the government, but they could never succeed. Even though they did not believe that Jesus was the true Messiah, they tried to get Him to show them a special sign. Matthew 16:2-3 tells us the story, He replied, "When evening comes, you say, 'It will be fair weather, for the sky is red,' and in the morning, 'Today it will be stormy, for the sky is red and overcast.' You know how to interpret the appearance of the sky, but you cannot interpret the signs of the times."

What Jesus is saying is that they could tell the coming weather but they could not tell the coming spiritual things. In fact, they couldn't even tell that it was the TRUE Messiah who was standing right before their eyes. Jesus wants us to be tuned into the spiritual things of the future. Matthew 24:42, "Therefore keep watch, because you do not know on what day your Lord will come."

Again, this author believes that the coming of Christ is *imminen*t pronounced (im-ma-nent). That means that the coming of Jesus could happen at any time. In Matthew 24:42 when Jesus says that we do not know what day Jesus will come, that tells us that there is no prophecy, in the author's opinion, left to be fulfilled in the Bible to keep Jesus from coming today, tonight, this week or this year. Be ready!

HINTS AND CLUES TO JESUS COMING

Even the disciples were confused about when Jesus would return! In Matthew 24:3 we are told, "As Jesus was sitting on the Mount of Olives, the disciples came to him privately. 'Tell us,' they said, "when will this happen, and what will be the sign of your coming and of the end of the age?" The disciples wanted to know.

What did Jesus tell us would be some hints and clues that His coming was getting closer?

People would be living ordinary lives and making fun of Jesus Coming

Matthew 24:37-39 "As it was in the days of Noah, so it will be at the coming of the Son of Man. For in the days before the flood, people were eating and drinking, marrying and giving in marriage, up to the day Noah entered the ark; and they knew nothing about what would happen until the flood came and took them all away. That is how it will be at the coming of the Son of Man."

The people in Noah's day lived ordinary lives, eating, laughing, marrying and working. They laughed at Noah and didn't really think the flood was coming. Jesus said that in the last days, people will be doing all those same things; living life as usual until Jesus comes in the flash of a moment.

People will deny that Jesus will return

2 Peter 3:3-4 states, "First of all, you must understand that in the last days scoffers will come, scoffing and following their own evil desires. They will say, "Where is this 'coming' he promised? Ever since our fathers died, everything goes on as it has since the beginning of creation."

More and more wars and rumors of war

Matthew 24:6 says, "You will hear of wars and rumors of wars, but see to it that you are not alarmed. Such things must happen, but the end is still to come." There have always been wars and rumors of wars but the Bible says they will get closer and closer together like the labor pains of a mother just before giving birth to a child.

Big battles will take place

Matthew 24:7 states, "Nation will rise against nation, and kingdom against kingdom."

Even though we don't know when Jesus is coming back, He did give us some road signs to be looking for so we can be aware that His coming is closer every day. Even the next to the last verse in the Bible talks about the coming of Christ. Revelation 22:20 says, "He who testifies to these things says, 'Yes I am coming soon.' Amen. Come Lord Jesus."

End Times in Easy Terms

Although we do not know when He is coming back, the sure thing is that the Bible teaches us that He IS coming back.

On March 11, 1942 on Corregidor Island a 62 yr old army officer with his family slipped away from the Philippines and made their way down to Australia. Before leaving the Islands, Gen. Douglas MacArthur said, "I will return." Two and one half years later on October 20, 1944 he stood again on the soil of the Philippines and said, "This is the voice of freedom. People of the Philippines, I have returned."

If you think a man can have that kind of credibility, and if you can appreciate that quality in a man, the Bible tells us today that Jesus Christ the God-man has made the same promise and is far more credible than any human being. He is coming again!

End Times in Easy Terms

Study Questions

1. Would you WANT to know the time of Jesus return if you could? Why or why not?

___

___

___

2. What did Jesus tell the disciples when they asked about the times and dates of His return?

___

___

3. How long have date setters and people proclaiming that Jesus has returned been around?

___

___

4. What are four principles or guidelines that scripture lays out for us to know about the rapture?

___

___

___

___

5. Look at Appendix B. What is the most surprising thing or shocking date setter to you throughout this list?

6. What are some events that Jesus Himself gave us to let us know that the timing of His return is getting closer? How has this changed over the years?

End Times in Easy Terms

> *For the Son of man shall come in the glory of his Father with his angels; and then He shall reward every man according to his works.*
> — Jesus

Chapter 5

What will happen at the Rapture?

When we talk about Jesus coming back in the air for His people there are naturally a lot of questions that arise. Here is a look at a few of those questions.

HOW WILL THE RAPTURE HAPPEN?

Perhaps the best known verse to describe what the rapture will be like is 1 Thessalonians 4:16-17, "For the Lord himself will come down from heaven, with a loud command, with the voice of the archangel and with the trumpet call of God, and the dead in Christ will rise first. After that, we who are still alive and are left will be caught up together with them in the clouds to meet the Lord in the air. And so we will be with the Lord forever."

We are told in these verses that:

JESUS IS COMING IN THE AIR:
- Jesus Himself will come down from heaven and He will stop somewhere up in the sky. Jesus will not actually touch foot on the earth at the rapture. We will talk about this later in this chapter.
- There will be an archangel (the highest ranking angel) proclaiming Jesus' arrival
- A trumpet blast will sound announcing the arrival of the Lord

In 1 Thessalonians 4:17 the phrase "shall be caught up" in the Greek language means to be "seized" or taken away. In this case Paul was talking about going to heaven with Jesus. That's a good thing!

Jesus will not set foot on the earth until after the great tribulation described in Revelation. At the Rapture we will be seized up at the same time, as the Greek language says.

If we can let our minds wander for a moment we might ask a fun question: How close to earth will Jesus come during the rapture? I know my immediate thought was "who cares?" But Paul does say that "we will meet the Lord in the air." A great Greek Scholar has some interesting insight on this thought.

End Times in Easy Terms

According to the Greek language there are two words for "air." The Greek word *aer* refers to the lower denser atmosphere. If the Greeks were speaking of a higher area where the air is thinner they would use the word *aither*.

If a Greek were on top of Mt. Olympus, 6,403feet high, (the highest point they knew) below him the air would be called *aer* and looking up above him the air would be called *aither* symbolizing a lower and higher atmosphere respectively. So which word did Paul use?

We see in 1 Thessalonians 4:13-18 Paul used the word *aer* to indicate that Christ's rapture might occur within the lower atmosphere of the earth. I would not stake my faith on what distance from the earth the rapture will happen, but it is interesting to note the Greek word Paul used. It is just a thought for contemplation and discussion. Have fun with that one.

JESUS IS COMING IN AUTHORITY:

2 Thessalonians 1:7 tells us "the Lord Jesus is revealed from heaven in blazing fire with his powerful angels. He will punish those who do not know God and do not obey the gospel of our Lord Jesus. They will be punished with everlasting destruction and shut out from the presence of the Lord"

You see friends; Jesus won't be coming as a baby, but a KING with a scepter of authority in His hand. He will not be in a manger but He will be riding a White Horse. He will not be wrapped in swaddling clothes but He will have a golden sash around his chest that says KING OF KINGS AND LORD OF LORDS...because His rapture coming will be in authority (Revelation 19:16.)

JESUS IS COMING WITH HIS ANGELS IN GREAT GLORY:

Matthew 16:27, "For the Son of Man is going to come in his Father's glory with his angels" Mark 8:38, "If anyone is ashamed of me and my words in this adulterous and sinful generation, the Son of Man will be ashamed of him when he comes in his Father's glory with the holy angels." Can you imagine the entire millions of angels in the air as you go up in the twinkling of an eye? Millions of them!

JESUS IS COMING WITH THOSE ALREADY THERE:

1 Thessalonians 4:14, says "We believe that Jesus died and rose again and so we believe that God will bring with Jesus those who have fallen asleep in him." The early Christians used the words "fall asleep" for death. They were not denying death but they knew that death was not the end of life. In fact, we ourselves never die, just our bodies.

So when Christians die before the Lord comes back, they themselves (that is their soul and spirit) are already in heaven with Jesus but their bodies are still dead.

My grandparents and dad and Christian friends will greet me! Those you know who are already in heaven will greet you if you are a Christian as you rise in the air!

HOW FAST WILL IT HAPPEN?

We are told from several scriptures about how quickly the rapture will happen.

Revelation 16:15, "Behold, I come like a thief!"

Matthew 24:27, "For as lightning that comes from the east is visible even in the west, so will be the coming of the Son of Man." We have already discussed this but it will be like lightning, a split second and it gone.

1 Corinthians 15:51-52 Paul tells us, "Listen, I tell you a mystery: We will not all sleep, but we will all be changed— in a flash, in the twinkling of an eye, at the last trumpet. For the trumpet will sound, the dead will be raised imperishable, and we will be changed."

This verse tells us how fast it will happen "In a moment, in the twinkling of an eye." That word "moment" is the Greek word "atomos" (atom) which means something that is so short or small it is indivisible or un-cuttable. It is as if it happens in an atom of time.

Matthew 24:27 tells us "For as lightning that comes from the east is visible even in the west, so will be the coming of the Son of Man." That is fast!

End Times in Easy Terms

Luke 12:39-40, "But understand this: If the owner of the house had known at what hour the thief was coming, he would not have let his house be broken into. You also must be ready, because the Son of Man will come at an hour when you do not expect him."

To make it simple, Jesus' return will be so quick and fast that no one will be able to measure it in time. This is further proven by the phrase "twinkling of an eye," which means the quick jerk of an eye or light hitting the eye. So how fast will it be? Just as fast as a lightning strike and then it's over.

HIS COMING WILL BE SIMILAR TO HIS LEAVING

In Acts 1:11 it says, "Men of Galilee, they said, why do you stand here looking into the sky? This same Jesus, who has been taken from you into heaven, will come back in the same way you have seen him go into heaven."

We are told that:

- Jesus will come back in the air like He left
- Jesus will come back in the form of a human body like He left
- Believers will recognize Jesus when He comes back just as the disciples knew who He was when He left

End Times in Easy Terms

WHAT DOES 'THE DEAD IN CHRIST WILL RISE FIRST' MEAN?

The Bible tells us in this verse that those Christians who have died before the rapture happens will be in heaven, (that is their spirit), but their bodies will still be in the grave. The phrase 'The dead in Christ rising first' talks about the bodies rising from the grave. The bodies will miraculously be perfected and reunited with their spirit in heaven.

The Bible never says if the graves will bust open or if they will "look undisturbed." I personally think the cemeteries will look no different after the rapture than before because the bodies will be a spiritual perfected body. The bodies will be raised by Christ and He does not need to move dirt to raise the dead in Christ.

WHAT ABOUT THOSE PEOPLE WHO ARE ALIVE WHEN THE RAPTURE HAPPENS?

Our verse in 1 Thessalonians 4:16-17 tells us that those of us who are alive will be caught up in the air. In other words we will be instantly changed and transformed into a perfected spirit, soul and body. We are told about this as well in 1 Corinthians 15:52-53, "In a moment, in the twinkling of an eye, at the last trump: for the trumpet shall sound, and the dead shall be raised incorruptible, and we shall be changed."

Paul contrasts what happens to the dead and to the living. We are told again that the Christians who have died first will be raised with a perfected body (incorruptible) and we will be changed. It all happens in the "twinkling of an eye."

WILL EVERYONE IN THE WORLD SEE THE RAPTURE AND KNOW WHAT HAPPENED?

Again, let us look at these verses. Matthew 24:27 tells us how fast it might happen, "For as lightning that comes from the east is visible even in the west, so will be the coming of the Son of Man."

Luke 17:24 "For the Son of Man in his day will be like the lightning, which flashes and lights up the sky from one end to the other."

We have already seen in these verses how quickly Jesus' coming will be, in an "atom" of time. The rapture of Jesus is not a long event that is played out like a parade. All of a sudden it happens and then millions of people are gone.

Perhaps people will hear something or see a glimpse of light but according to the Bible, it will be so fast that they will not be able to watch the whole thing and know what is happening. It will be just too fast. When it happens I believe there will be mass confusion because of the millions of missing believers.

End Times in Easy Terms

WHAT IS THE DIFFERENCE BETWEEN THE RAPTURE AND THE SECOND COMING?

This is a great question that so many people are confused about. Many times these two terms are used as the same event, but they are not.

The Bible is very clear on the issue of the second coming. The Bible says that Jesus will return to earth (the second coming) 1260 days from the day the Antichrist establishes himself in the temple and declares himself to be God. In Revelation 11:3 we are told "And I will give power to my two witnesses, and they will prophesy for 1260 days, clothed in sackcloth".

We see the Bible clearly stating an unknown date for the Rapture (meeting Jesus in the air), Mark 13:31-33, "Heaven and earth will pass away, but my words will never pass away. No one knows about that day or hour, not even the angels in heaven, nor the Son, but only the Father. Be on guard! Be alert! You do not know when that time will come."

So the Bible states an unknown date (the rapture) and a known date, (the second coming). Many scholars have logically concluded that there must be two different events occurring--the rapture and the second coming.

End Times in Easy Terms

Study Questions

1. What is the most famous passage describing the rapture?

2. Where will the believers meet Jesus in the rapture?

3. Is Jesus coming alone or will there be others with Him in the air?

4. How quickly does the Bible say that the rapture will happen?

5. Do you think Jesus will appear in the rapture over Israel? Why or why not?

End Times in Easy Terms

6. What is the difference between the rapture and the second coming?

___

___

___

___

7. What are we told to do in Mark 13:31-33?

___

___

8. What do you think about the thoughts on the possibility of how close Jesus will come to the earth at the rapture?

___

___

> "Speculations? I know nothing about speculations. I'm resting on certainties. I know that my Redeemer lives, and because He lives, I shall live also."
>
> Scientist Michael Faraday

CHAPTER 6

WHAT WILL OUR BODIES BE LIKE IN HEAVEN?

Whether a person dies before the rapture happens or if they are alive when the rapture happens, the Bible specifically tells us that we will have a renewed or perfect body. Many scriptures encourage us with this information.

Let's talk about what happens to believers who die before the rapture takes place. Again, look at the important following verses.

End Times in Easy Terms

The Bible tells us plainly about those who die before the rapture in 1 Thessalonians 4:13-18, "Brothers, we do not want you to be ignorant about those who fall asleep *(die)*, or to grieve like the rest of men, who have no hope. We believe that Jesus died and rose again and so we believe that God will bring with Jesus those who have fallen asleep *(died)* in him. According to the Lord's own word, we tell you that we who are still alive, who are left till the coming of the Lord, will certainly not precede those who have fallen asleep *(died)*. For the Lord himself will come down from heaven, with a loud command, with the voice of the archangel and with the trumpet call of God, and the dead in Christ will rise first. After that, we who are still alive and are left will be caught up together with them in the clouds to meet the Lord in the air. And so we will be with the Lord forever. Therefore encourage each other with these words."

In 1 Corinthians 15:51-53 Paul gives us a clue as to what our bodies are going to be like in heaven, "Listen, I tell you a mystery: We will not all sleep *(die)*, but we will all be changed— in a flash, in the twinkling of an eye, at the last trumpet. For the trumpet will sound, the dead will be raised imperishable, and we will be changed. For the perishable must clothe itself with the imperishable and the mortal with immortality." He tells us that our bodies will not decay (imperishable) and we will never die again (immortal).

End Times in Easy Terms

In 1 Thessalonians 4:13-18 and 1 Corinthians 15:51-53 the word "sleep" means "death" or to "die." I have included the word "die" in italics to bring the clearer message out in the verses. In the early days Christians knew that death was not the end so they used the word "sleep" to denote that there is a resurrection and eternal "awakeness" for the believers. In other words we will be alive and awake forever with God in heaven. We will not just lie in the grave for all eternity.

Both verses tell us that the spirit of those Christians who die before Jesus comes back; go on to be with God in heaven while their bodies stay buried in the ground. They are still the same person, waiting in heaven, but as spiritual beings without a physical body until the rapture.

WHAT? I WON'T HAVE A BODY IN HEAVEN BEFORE THE RAPTURE HAPPENS???

How can we remain alive without a physical body? That's a good question. The first thing we have to understand is HOW God made us. So let's talk about that a minute. The Bible tells us that we are made up of at least three aspects. Let's consider the following verses.

1 Thessalonians 5:23 "May God himself, the God of peace, sanctify you through and through. May your whole spirit,

soul and body be kept blameless at the coming of our Lord Jesus Christ."

Hebrews 4:12 "For the word of God is living and active. Sharper than any double-edged sword, it penetrates even to dividing soul and spirit, joints and marrow"

FIRST: YOU ARE A LIVING SOUL WITH PERSONALITY

When we first look at how God made humans (Adam) Genesis 2:7 tells us "the LORD God formed the man from the dust of the ground and breathed into his nostrils the breath of life, and the man became a living being." The word for "being" is "soul." The fact that God created us as a soul simply means that we are alive. So first and foremost you are a spiritual SOUL, a living being.

In fact we are told that every living human is a soul and every soul (or person) is responsible for their decision toward God. In Ezekiel 18:4 we read, "For every living soul belongs to me, the father as well as the son—both alike belong to me. The soul who sins is the one who will die."

We are also told that animals have souls, living bodies given life by God. In Leviticus 17:11 we are told about the life (soul) of an animal is in the blood and when you take the blood the soul or life is gone, "For the life of a creature is in the blood, and I have given it to you to make atonement for yourselves on the altar; it is the blood that makes atonement for one's life."

End Times in Easy Terms

The sacrifice of the life (soul) of a creature made atonement for a human's life (soul.) So the Bible tells us that both humans and animals have souls because they are alive. You have a soul because you are alive.

The word for "soul" in the Greek language is "psuche" pronounced (psoo-khay). This is where we get our word "Psyche" which we use for "psychology," dealing with the mind and emotions of a person. It is our soul or "psyche" that gives us personality. How our personality is developed is dependent on our parents, the DNA we receive at conception and our upbringing.

Again the Bible tells us that even animals have a soul. Animals, as most of us know and realize have a personality, they are not just robots. They can love, play, get aggressive, think and reason to some degree. It is this soul that gives both humans and animals their own personality. We have life and personality because we have a soul, given by God.

Let me explain it a little more. You see, Adam and Eve were in the Garden of Eden and everything was perfect. God gave Adam a warning when he said "in the day you eat of the tree you will die." God kept His promise, Adam ate from the tree and in that day Adam died. If Adam died then why was he still alive? Because he didn't die physically, he died spiritually. He was still alive and he had a body (and he still had his own personality) after he sinned, but he died spiritually. He was still a spiritual being but his *spirit* needed to be renewed because he sinned.

Adam was now like us; he had a soul (because he was alive), he had a body and he had a spirit that needed to be renewed. Everyone has a soul which means that we are alive and have a personality.

SECOND: YOU HAVE A BODY

Just like Adam, we have a body. Our body is what God breathed our soul into. Our body is what physically keeps us alive, but who we are is really our soul and spirit. My name is Dan Ingram but the real Dan is not what I look like on the outside! (Boy am I grateful for that!) I am a living soul and spirit! Our soul means that we have life and being and that gives us importance as it comes from God.

Your physical body, the body you now have, is only to keep you alive here on this earth. You need your lungs to process oxygen, your heart to move the blood around in your body, your brain to process everything your body does and all your other organs to keep you alive. Your body is NOT who you are, your body only keeps the REAL YOU alive.

Our bodies are good, God gave us our bodies and we need to honor God with everything we are including our bodies as we are told in 1 Corinthians 6:20 "You were bought at a price. Therefore honor God with your body."

End Times in Easy Terms

But neither your body, nor your soul, nor your spirit will be permanently gone in the future. God has a plan for your body, soul and spirit. We'll examine that in a bit.

THIRD: YOU HAVE A SPIRIT

The Bible tells us that we ARE a living soul but we HAVE a spirit. Every person has a spirit! Numbers 16:22 says, "But Moses and Aaron fell face down and cried out, "O God, God of the spirits of all mankind, will you be angry with the entire assembly when only one man sins?"

Everyone is born with a spirit but our spirit is disconnected from God. Our sinful disconnected spirit is why Jesus came to die for us. It is our spirit that connects with God. Animals have a soul (they are alive with personality) and a body but they have no spirit. Animals cannot connect in a spiritual manner with God, but you can.

The Bible tells us that the real us, who we are, is both soul and spirit contained in our body. We are spiritual beings.

SO. . . WHAT HAPPENS TO OUR BODIES AFTER WE GO TO HEAVEN?

Now, let's get back to our question…WHAT? I WON'T HAVE A BODY? Well, if a Christian dies before Jesus comes back the Bible tells us in 2 Corinthians 5:8, "We are confident, I say, and would prefer to be away from the body and at home with the Lord. So we make it our goal to please him, whether we are at home in the body or away from it."

Paul tells us that we will be at home in heaven even if we don't have a body! We will all be OK because as spiritual beings, being a soul and spirit, we don't need a body. Remember our earthly body was only to keep us alive on earth. As soul and spirit we are spiritual beings. No, we won't be naked without bodies because we will be spiritual beings! But there is still a future for our earthly bodies. They will not be gone forever.

1 Thessalonians 4:13-18 tells us much information about what will happen to our bodies both after we die and when we are alive at the return of Jesus. Let's take 1 Thessalonians verse by verse and see what we can learn.

Verse 14: Jesus will bring back those who have previously died before the Rapture. When we depart in death and are away from our body we are still us! We will be in heaven and come back with Jesus in the air at the rapture. But something special will happen to those who come back with Jesus.

Verse 15: The special thing that happens to all our bodies will FIRST happen to those who have died and now are coming back with Jesus.

Verse 16: The surprise; Those who are with Jesus in the air, their physical bodies that were previously buried in cemeteries or cremated or lost will supernaturally reform, come back together, appear and instantly become new renewed physical bodies that will be reunited with their soul and spirit and they will be a complete perfected bodies, souls and spirits once again.

Verse 17: Those who are still alive on the earth when the rapture happens will be caught up together with Jesus in the air. I want to remind us of 1 Corinthians 15:51-53 as it tells us what will happen to our bodies: "Listen, I tell you a mystery: We will not all sleep, but we will all be changed— in a flash, in the twinkling of an eye, at the last trumpet. For the trumpet will sound, the dead will be raised imperishable, and we will be changed. For the perishable must clothe itself with the imperishable and the mortal with immortality." Did you hear that? We won't all die but we will all be changed. The dead will be changed and the living will be changed. We will all have a soul, spirit and a perfected body. If we were sick here on earth, we will be healthy. If we had something wrong with us like a disease or blindness, or a hand or foot missing or trouble speaking or walking or thinking or cancer or anything at all, they will be made perfect at the rapture. It will all happen in a flash, in an atom of time!

Our new bodies will be totally different kind of bodies. They will be perfect bodies that will never get sick, or hurt or die ever again. The word "imperishable" means to "never decay." In heaven we will never grow old. Our bodies will be perfect forever.

End Times in Easy Terms

<u>WILL WE KNOW EACH OTHER IN HEAVEN?</u>

What would it be like to be in heaven with millions of strangers? We will not be strangers. The Bible teaches that we will all know each other. Paul understood this when he was teaching the Corinthian believers about this in 1 Corinthians 13:12 "Now I know in part; then I shall know fully, even as I am fully known." Paul knew that in heaven we will know each other even as people know us.

Jesus' disciples recognized Him many times after the resurrection. In Jesus' perfected resurrected body he was still a guy, still had his same bodily features and looked like Himself before He was resurrected. He was still recognized as JESUS!

At Jesus' Transfiguration Peter, James and John were there and the Bible tells us that the disciples recognized Moses and Elijah even though they couldn't have known what they looked like because Moses lived 1400 years before the disciples and Elijah lived 800 years before. But the disciples knew, recognized and acknowledged two men with Jesus, who still had their earthly names; Moses and Elijah and still retained their male gender. I believe we will instantly KNOW people we have not previously met. How much fun it will be to see our family and friends who are there too!

The Bible never talks about our total memory being completely wiped away. In fact 1 Thessalonians 4:14-18 says we'll all be together in heaven and to comfort each other with that fact. What comfort would there be in getting to heaven and not even recognizing or knowing your loved ones or friends? In many verses the Bible teaches there will be a great reunion in heaven. 1 Thessalonians 2:19-20 "For what is our hope, our joy, or the crown in which we will glory in the presence of our Lord Jesus when he comes? Is it not you? Indeed, you are our glory and joy." The joy we have in heaven with our friends and family is just part of what God gives us when we are there in heaven together. We could go on and on about the longing Paul has for those he ministered to here on earth that he is looking forward to seeing in heaven when he gets there.

WILL I STILL BE A MALE OR FEMALE OR DO I CHANGE INTO AN ANGEL?

Angels are created beings. They are a separate creation. We will not turn into angels in heaven. We will still be who we are here on earth, just with a perfected body, soul and spirit as we have talked about earlier. The Bible shows us that we will still retain our male or female gender. Remember; Jesus was still Jesus after the resurrection. Moses and Elijah were still men and themselves and even had their earthly given names after being in heaven for over 1400 years and 800 years. You will still be you!

End Times in Easy Terms

WHAT ABOUT MY ETHNIC RACE, CULTURE, HERITAGE OR SKIN COLOR?

Revelation 5:9-10 says "and with your blood you purchased men for God from every tribe and language and people and nation. You have made them to be a kingdom and priests to serve our God, and they will reign on the earth." Revelation 7:9 "After this I looked and there before me was a great multitude that no one could count, from every nation, tribe, people and language, standing before the throne and in front of the Lamb. They were wearing white robes and were holding palm branches in their hands."

When John was writing Revelation he was in exile on the Isle of Patmos. However he tells us in Revelation 4:1-2 that God brought him up into heaven and John was in the spirit, "After this I looked, and there before me was a door standing open in heaven. And the voice I had first heard speaking to me like a trumpet said, "Come up here, and I will show you what must take place after this." ²At once I was in the Spirit, and there before me was a throne in heaven with someone sitting on it." John was taken into heaven by God for this vision. In heaven John sees so many people that he said you cannot even count them all. But of all the people, he saw different nations, tribes, people and languages. How did John know? Because they looked different! Their skin color was different. Their facial features were different.

End Times in Easy Terms

The Bible tells us that we will retain our skin color, ethnicity and heritage. Why wouldn't we? After all the Psalmist tells us in Psalm 139:14 that we are "fearfully and wonderfully made" by God and what God created us to be will still carry on into Heaven!

Interestingly enough John even said that there were different languages in Heaven. Maybe we will continue to speak the language we were raised with. Perhaps we will be able to speak and understand each other's different languages or perhaps there will be a heavenly language but the Bible is clear to delineate there are different tribes, nations, people and languages in heaven.

HOW OLD WILL I BE IN HEAVEN?

We have to understand, that because we live here on earth we live IN time. Gravity, disease, stress and age all take a toll on our bodies and we grow one year older while we live. But in heaven there is no time.

Our bodies have age but our spirits are ageless! When we get to heaven we will live OUTSIDE of time because heaven is forever, or infinity. We will never grow old because time as we know it will not exist. There will be no age in heaven. We will not grow old; we will be spiritual beings without age.

End Times in Easy Terms

IF I AM STILL ME, WHAT WILL I DO IN HEAVEN, SIT AND PLAY THE HARP FOR ETERNITY?

Revelation 7:15 tells us that saints will be serving God before His throne but it will not be tiresome. David says in Psalm 16:11 "In Your presence there is nothing but joy." Whatever we do it will be joyous! Jesus told the parable of the ten minas in Luke 19 teaching us about working while the master is gone. We have to work and invest with what we have been given. But when the master comes back there will be an accounting, he will put those who did well in charge of many things. Jesus is telling us what we do as believers on this earth will have a direct impact on what we do and the responsibilities we are given in Heaven. In Heaven there will be different positions, leadership and responsibilities.

If each of us are given gifts of the Spirit for the common good here on earth, we have no reason to think that will end when we get to heaven. I believe we will still be using our gifts in heaven, just as we did here on the earth.

Not only will there be good works and service in Heaven but there will be singing and music in heaven. Read Psalm 104:33 and Revelation 8:7ff, 15:2.

The Bible tells us that there will be nations and governments and kings. Revelation 21:24 "The nations will walk by its light, and the kings of the earth will bring their splendor into it." Revelation 21:26 tells us that "the glory and honor of the nations will be brought into it." Revelation 22:2 says "the leaves of the tree are for the healing of the nations."

Kings, nations, languages, tribes, order, work, singing, music and all those things that we are used to here on earth, will be seen in heaven. But there is one difference between those things on earth and in Heaven; up in Heaven they will all be perfect and fulfilling. We will not get tired because all our work will be for the purpose of serving God and fulfilling His agenda for us.

Heaven will not be sitting on a cloud playing a harp for all eternity, but it will be a journey. We are even told that God made the "heavens" new. Perhaps we'll get to explore all of God's creation even in outer space!

Study Questions

1. The Bible tells us that we are made up of three parts. What are they?

___

2. What part gives us our personality and what part relates to God in terms of salvation?

___

End Times in Easy Terms

3. How can we stay alive in heaven if we do not have a physical body before the resurrection?

_____

_____

_____

4. How does that make you feel knowing that you will still be exactly you, perfect and without sin, when you get to heaven?

_____

_____

_____

5. Why is it important to know that the Bible teaches that we will know each other and be known by others when we get to heaven?

_____

_____

_____

6. What do you think you will be doing when you get to heaven?

_____

_____

_____

End Times in Easy Terms

> "There are two kinds of people: those who say to God, "Thy will be done," and those to whom God says, "All right, then, have it your way."
>
> C.S. Lewis

Chapter 7

A Brief Look at the Tribulation

Again I must advise the reader that this book is not a scholarly study on the end times, the book of Revelation or the tribulation. The tribulation is a VERY difficult topic to address, study, understand and teach. There are numerous interpretations, ways to look at it, symbolisms, numbers, visions and ideas on the book of Revelation and especially the tribulation.

Please understand that I realize and respect the other viewpoints of those who may disagree with the premise of my ideas on the tribulation. However with that being said I will again present my more conservative and more literal interpretation and ideas as I see the tribulation playing out.

I believe the best that we can do is see the big picture of the tribulation although many even argue over that. We start getting confused when we get down to the smaller interpretations as to what numbers mean what and what does this vision symbolize or is Revelation even in chronological order. If you ask ten different scholars you will probably get eleven different answers.

I am going to stay away from guessing about the very confusing interpretations. If you have specific questions you can go online, study commentaries, or ask your Pastor or Sunday School teacher.

WHAT IS THE TRIBULATION?

In a nutshell, the tribulation is taught by Bible Scholars to be a seven year period in which God finalizes His promises to the nation of Israel and brings final judgment upon the earth of satan and his followers. The word "tribulation" in the dictionary has this meaning, "a grievous trouble, severe trial or suffering. An affliction."

We do not have to read through Revelation very far to get the idea that during the days of the tribulation it will certainly be a time of severe trouble, trial and suffering. In fact the New Testament tells us in Matthew 24:21, "For then there will be great distress, unequaled from the beginning of the world until now, and never to be equaled again." In no uncertain terms we are told it will be the worst time on earth in all of human history and will never be equaled again.

WHEN WILL THE TRIBULATION START?

Although many differ on this, I believe that the tribulation will begin after the rapture happens. Whether that is immediately or when the antichrist signs the false peace treaty in Daniel 9:27 at some period after, I do not think anyone knows for sure.

However, it looks like it will happen AFTER the rapture. Let us look at 2 Thessalonians 2. In this chapter, Paul is teaching the people that the antichrist or the man of lawlessness has not come, as rumors were spreading. He makes it very clear that the man will be revealed BUT something must happen first.

2 Thessalonians 2:3-4, "Don't let anyone deceive you in any way, for ‹that day will not come› until the rebellion occurs and the man of lawlessness is revealed, the man doomed to destruction. He will oppose and will exalt himself over everything that is called God or is worshiped, so that he sets himself up in God's temple, proclaiming himself to be God." Paul teaches that this cannot happen until something else happens first. There must be a removing of the force that holds him back.

2 Thessalonians 2:6-8 tells us about that event that precedes the coming of the man of lawlessness, "And now you

know what is holding him back, so that he may be revealed at the proper time. For the secret power of lawlessness is already at work; but the one who now holds it back will continue to do so till he is taken out of the way. And then the lawless one will be revealed." According to this verse, it seems to teach that the One who holds him back, is the Holy Spirit residing in the hearts of all believers and until He is removed (the rapture) this evil man will not be revealed. Therefore the Bible seems to show us that believers probably will not see the antichrist, this man of lawlessness because he is revealed after the rapture. That means we can all stop guessing!

SO WHAT ARE THE SPECIFIC PURPOSES FOR THE GREAT TRIBULATION ON EARTH?

The Bible distinguishes general tribulations (trials, troubles, afflictions on the earth) from the Great Tribulation. The Great Tribulation is a definite period at the end of the age in Matthew 24:29-35 and it is called the "Great Tribulation" in Revelation 7:14.

In the big picture, the Great Tribulation generally has a threefold purpose:

(1) to end "the times of the Gentiles" Luke 21:24 "They will fall by the sword and will be taken as prisoners to all the nations. Jerusalem will be trampled on by the Gentiles until the times of the Gentiles are fulfilled."

(2) Worldwide Evangelism: This purpose is given and fulfilled in Revelation 7:1-17. During the first half of the tribulation, God will evangelize the world by the means of the 144,000 Jews and thus fulfill the prophecy found in Matthew 24:14. Also, an angel will preach "an eternal gospel . . . to those who live on the earth and to every nation and tribe and tongue and people" (Revelation 14:6).

(3) To show once and for all, to satan and his followers who try to rule one final time and destroy all that God has created, that Jehovah God is sovereign and supreme over ALL THINGS!

This great battle takes place, obviously on the earth, so that is where the tribulation takes place. If we can look at it this way, seven represents God's perfect number of completion. The seven years of the Great Tribulation represents God's perfect judgment or refinement of the earth.

The Bible tells us that it will be a time when the nations of the world will try to destroy Israel and even the antichrist sets himself up in the temple in Jerusalem. It will be a horrible time for the nation of Israel and the Jews. Zechariah 12:3, "On that day, when all the nations of the earth are gathered against her, I will make Jerusalem an immovable rock for all the nations. All who try to move it will injure themselves."

The nations in Ezekiel 38-39 are commonly held by some scholars to be Russia and her allies, perhaps the Islamic world to be the attack on Israel. Jesus talks in Matthew 24 how terrible the days of the tribulation will be for Israel and others going through the terrible ordeal.

The Old Testament writers call this time of tribulation by different names: "The Time of Jacob's Trouble" Jeremiah 30:7 says "How awful that day will be! None will be like it. It will be a time of trouble for Jacob, but he will be saved out of it." It is called the "Time of Distress" Daniel 12:1 "At that time Michael, the great prince who protects your people, will arise. There will be a time of distress such as has not happened from the beginning of nations until then." Malachi calls it "the Day of His coming" in Malachi 3:2 "But who can endure the day of his coming? Who can stand when he appears? For he will be like a refiner's fire or a launderer's soap."

We see that God will bring Israel through the tribulation but it will be a very difficult time.

WILL CHRISTIANS HAVE TO GO THROUGH THE TRIBULATION?

That is a hotly debated question for a lot of people. Only briefly, here, will I share a few major differing thoughts on the tribulation and how the rapture might fit. There are basically three major views on the rapture and the tribulation. Whatever tribulation rapture view you hold, will determine if you believe that Christians will go through the tribulation or not.

1. PRE-TRIBULATION RAPTURE. This is the interpretation from which I am teaching. This view teaches that the rapture of Christ will happen BEFORE the tribulation starts and that the rapture ushers in the beginning of the seven years of tribulation on earth.

There are many verses in the Bible that tell us that believers will not have to go through or face the coming judgment or wrath. The clearest one is found in the little book of 1 Thessalonians 1:10 "to wait for his Son from heaven, whom he raised from the dead—Jesus, who rescues us from the coming wrath."

Romans 5:9, "Since we have now been justified by his blood, how much more shall we be saved from God's wrath through him!"

There is no verse in the Bible that specifically states the rapture will happen BEFORE the tribulation. There are some people who take the same verses that seem to teach a pre-tribulation rapture and they see them as teaching a mid or post-tribulation rapture. To be sure, there are certainly no unmistakable proof texts that teach the absolute way that it will happen.

2. MID-TRIBULATION RAPTURE. This view teaches that the church (believers) will go through the first three and one

half years of the tribulation. This will be a period of false peace between the world and Israel.

The end time prophecy in Daniel tells us this in 9:27 "He will confirm a covenant with many for one 'seven.' In the middle of the 'seven' he will put an end to sacrifice and offering. And on a wing ‹of the temple› he will set up an abomination that causes desolation, until the end that is decreed is poured out on him."

This verse tells us that the antichrist will make a treaty or "deal" with Israel for one period of seven. (This also represents a "*week*" if you want to study that further.) In the middle of the seven or three and one half, he will break the false peace treaty and set himself up in the Jewish temple as god until his end has come.

Mid-tribulation rapture theory teaches that when the antichrist breaks the false treaty and sets himself up as god, then the rapture of Christ will come.

3. POST-TRIBULATION RAPTURE. This view teaches that believers will be here on earth and go through the tribulation and then be raptured at the second coming of Christ. In other words, at the end of the tribulation the rapture happens, Christians are caught up in the air with Christ and then descend down to earth at the second coming when Christ sets His foot on earth the second time in history.

End Times in Easy Terms

Personally I believe the Christians will not go through the tribulation and that Christ is coming back in the rapture before the tribulation fulfilling the verse that the believers are not destined for His wrath. However, I heard a pastor say one time, "We all will be raptured according to our view!" In other words, no one knows exactly how it is going to happen.

WHO ARE THE MAJOR PLAYERS IN THE GREAT TRIBULATION?

There are a cast of players we read about in the book of Revelation. Again, certain interpretations may influence who you think these players are. Let us look at these one by one.

God: We see all through the Great Tribulation that no matter how bad things get that God is always in control. In fact we read over and over that through this ordeal God is constantly calling out to people to come to Him. This is not a vengeful God who delights in death. No! God is calling for the salvation of anyone who will come. We will look at those verses in chapter 8.

Jesus, the Lamb: Jesus is described as the victorious Lamb slain before the foundation of the world as our sacrifice for sins. He is the victor who eventually wins everything in the end!

The Sun Clothed Woman:

Revelation 12:1-2, "A great and wondrous sign appeared in heaven: a woman clothed with the sun, with the moon under her feet and a crown of twelve stars on her head. She was pregnant and cried out in pain as she was about to give birth."

Theologians have debated for ages her identity. It's not Mary since she gave birth to Christ on Earth not in heaven. Some think she stands for the Church but that idea does not fit the context. Israel, not the church gave birth to the Messiah, Jesus. Most theologians agree that the woman stands for Israel.

She is described as clothed with sun and moon so she is not just one real person. She is crowned with 12 stars (the 12 tribes of Israel) and Israel is often referred to as a woman in scripture. The fact that Israel is seen in heaven is a clue to us to see that God is still protecting the Nation of Israel. The physical nations (not just Jewish Christians) are still very important to God and end time.

There is something very unique about this woman (Israel); she is about to give birth. The emphasis in the Bible is on her pain and suffering. The meaning is that the faithful Jews, looking for the real Messiah has been suffering prior to the coming of Jesus.

The birth itself does not necessarily relate to the direct birth of Jesus but refers to the travail of the community from which the Messiah (Jesus) has come. It's always been hard for the followers of Jesus.

In Matthew 24 Jesus described what would happen to the Jewish people in the end times, not just Christians, but Jews in general and He talked about horrible things that would happen and in verse 8, He said these are the beginnings of birth pains. It will be hard to be a Jew and a Christian in the end.

Micah 4:10 "Writhe in agony, O Daughter of Zion, like a woman in labor, for now you must leave the city to camp in the open field. You will go to Babylon; there you will be rescued. There the LORD will redeem you out of the hand of your enemies."

Micah 5:3 Therefore Israel will be abandoned until the time when she who is in labor gives birth and the rest of his brothers return to join the Israelites."

The Child:

It is almost universally accepted that the male child here is referring to Jesus Christ Himself. She has the child and He is caught up.

There were so many incidents during the life of Christ where satan tried to destroy Jesus: the attempt of the crowd to throw Jesus over the cliff in Luke 4, satan asking Jesus to throw Himself off the temple and proving He really is God, and the ultimate, having Him crucified. Satan surely thought he had won.

But we know through the death and resurrection of Jesus Christ that satan lost and at the resurrection and ascension Jesus was taken up and satan lost the battle! Jesus is in heaven now at His throne and that's what verse 5 is talking about.

End Times in Easy Terms

The Two Witnesses:

There is great debate on who these 2 witnesses are. So let's look at it logically and biblically:

A. They are Persons. Nobody knows for sure WHO. Now I will tell you who I think they are. When the Rapture happens we know Paul said that we who are alive and remain will be caught up with Christ in the air. So there will be some people who will not die, they will change in the rapture. However, until the rapture happens, Hebrews 9:27 says everyone has to die once, then face the consequences.

Did you know that in all of history there have only been 2 people who have NOT died? Those two people were Enoch and Elijah, both in the Old Testament. Genesis 5:24 says that Enoch walked with God and was not. God just took him, he did not die. Speaking of Elijah in 2 Kings 2 God took him up in a whirlwind in a chariot of fire. These are the only 2 men in history that have not experienced death.

If Hebrews 9:27 is correct, and it is, I believe Enoch and Elijah are the 2 witnesses in Revelation 11 who will experience death the first time here on earth.

B. They are Prophets: Revelation 11:3, 6, 10 all these verses tell us they will prophesy. And God's enemies will hate them because they will prophesy for three and one half years.

C. They are Powerful: Revelation 11:3 God gave them power to do all kinds of things; To make it quit raining (Elijah did that while he was here on earth the first time) or to kill people with fire coming out of their mouth or to turn the water to blood or call down plagues. If you study Revelation you see during the whole first part of the Great Tribulation, plagues, water turning into blood and many other things. Biblically, we see these happening from God's perspective. But on the earth, it may appear to be the 2 witnesses causing this to happen. That is why they are hated by the WHOLE world.

D. They are Protected: God calls them the Olive Tree and Lamp Stand. Olive oil was what burned in the lamps. They were the light of God on the earth and the Olive Tree in the Bible is symbolic of the Holy Spirit. They are God's light and have His protective Spirit on them for a time.

Satan/ Red Dragon:

This is describing satan himself. When we study the end times and when reading through the book of Revelation, if we stay patient and continue to read, Revelation interprets a lot of what is in the book. The dragon is satan. Look at the description the Bible gives him.

Enormous meaning fierce in power

Red meaning murderous blood- thirsty character

7 Heads meaning wisdom. He is very wise but he has used that to fulfill his corrupt plans.

10 Horns meaning the symbol of power

7 Crowns meaning the symbol of authority

He is an evil king who was once called by Jesus, "the prince of this world." But he is king of a dying planet winding down to judgment and he will be judged one day.

Mighty tail taking 1/3 of the angels with him: When Lucifer decided HE wanted to be God, he was cast out of heaven. He went from the Angel of Light to the father of night, perfectly evil determined to battle the Lord God Almighty for control of the universe and he convinced one third of the angels that he could do it and they followed him. There are a HUGE number of demons working for satan.

Leonard Ravenhill, the great British evangelist once prayed, "Lord, we read where one third of the angels fell from heaven but praise God that means that two thirds didn't fall. Lord thank you that there are still two mighty angels for every wicked demon."

Satan is described lurking about in front of the woman (Israel) until the Messiah was born and then he tried to kill him. You see it was evil forces that inspired Pharaoh to kill all the male babies so that he might kill Moses. It was evil forces who inspired King Herod to murder all those babies so that he might kill Jesus. Satan was certainly lurking trying to defeat God by cutting off Israel and the Messiah.

Throughout history someone has always brought violence against the Jews. Here we find the origin of that hatred and why it is so evil. Satan was in the garden to try to destroy Adam and Eve but God covered them. Satan tried to destroy the Jewish race all through history but God covered, protected and delivered them. Revelation 12 is God's picture of how it all got started.

Notice the devil's influence; he leads the whole world astray. Now, I'm not one that sees a demon behind every bush, but I also don't dismiss the devil and demons as fantasy or allegorical.

There really is a devil and demons and they are out to try to destroy God's creation; you, me and everything that stands for good. It is very plain; he leads the whole world astray. Jesus said the devil was a liar from the beginning, and "he knows his time is short."

The Beast/ Antichrist:

Just as the word "rapture" is never mentioned in the Bible, people are surprised to learn that the term "antichrist" is not mentioned in the book of Revelation. The word "antichrist" is mentioned several other places in the New Testament but not in Revelation. When one puts the scriptures together and allows scripture to interpret scripture, we see the antichrist described in the book of Revelation.

Revelation 17:15 tells us, "Then the angel said to me, "The waters you saw, where the prostitute sits, are peoples, multitudes, nations and languages. The sea is the meaning for gentiles. The beast comes out of the non-Jewish background; he is going to be a gentile. Please understand when we say "BEAST" he's not a "beast" as we think. He is a man-a human, except he's controlled by satan. We call him a politician. I joke about that but the man controlled by satan we call the beast really is a politician.

If there was ever a man whose father was the devil this is the man. In Revelation 12:3 it tells us he has the likeness of a dragon! Satan. There is no mistaking his father, satan.

Satan always tries to mock and counterfeit God in many ways as we will see. When Jesus was on earth, Jesus said, "If you've seen Me, you've seen the Father." Jesus was a perfect example of God. This beast from the sea is the perfect example of his father the devil. The beast in essence will be able to say, if you've seen me, you've seen my father, the devil. He will say I and my father are one. Satan is a counterfeit of God.

This beast will be a pawn in the hand of satan and will have more power than all the successive world empires before him. In essence this beast (that is this man controlled by satan) is a composite of the four beasts in Daniel 7. A composite of the greatest leaders satan has ever had all rolled into one!

John 5:43 tells us the world will receive the antichrist wholeheartedly because they have rejected Jesus Christ. That is his family lineage.

End Times in Easy Terms

Jesus was victorious over sin, death and the grave and lives today to have a relationship with us if we will choose Him. So what does the devil do? He creates a FALSE affliction. Why is the beast so appealing? He mocks Christ's resurrection and deceives the people of the world. Look at what happens; He has a deadly wound that's been healed! You see again, the beast does not look like a hideous creature. It is his character, not his appearance. He is a man that is controlled by satan.

The Bible says the devil can even appear as an angel of light. Perhaps he will be witty, charming, charismatic, handsome, we don't know but he will be a man from the sea of people and be very persuasive.

This man will receive a deadly wound in the head and then be revived, rising to a world popularity that has never been known. John F. Kennedy's popularity went way up after his assassination, the same thing happened to Reagan. Years ago when the POPE was shot, he lived and the whole world wondered after him. This is what's going to happen to the man called the beast. He will be the world's benefactor.

Satan will finally get what he's always wanted; worldwide worship. The whole world asking "who is like this beast, who in the world can make war against him?"

2 Thessalonians 2:3-4 tells us "Don't let anyone deceive you in any way, for that day will not come until the rebellion occurs and the man of lawlessness is revealed, the man doomed to

End Times in Easy Terms

destruction. ⁴He will oppose and will exalt himself over everything that is called God or is worshiped, so that he sets himself up in God's temple, proclaiming himself to be God." In China millions worshipped Mao Tse Tung. In the 1940's many worshipped Hitler. Here in America we have all sorts of people following swamis and cult leaders who have convinced people that they are divine and worthy to be followed.

After the rapture when 144,000 Jews and countless numbers of gentiles come to faith in Jesus, the beast will wage war against them.

He is proud enough to blaspheme God and was given GLOBAL authority, unifying the world with a one world government. He will do it by dazzling some, dominating others and destroying yet others to get his own way. He establishes a one world religion worshipping the man the Bible calls the beast.

From the beginning of the early church, people have been accusing and guessing as to "who" the antichrist is. Jesus said "there are many antichrists" but who is the one? Who is that pawn in the hand of satan? Who is that man?

Some have thought that the antichrist may be more of a system, a country or power than an individual. Early church leaders thought the antichrist may be the line of Roman Caesars. I believe if you will dig deep enough probably every world leader at some point may have been considered the antichrist. Even

End Times in Easy Terms

President Ronald Wilson Reagan was a candidate because he had six letters in each of his names!

We are free to guess but it has to stop at conjecture. Many people are very adamant about whom they think the antichrist is but I believe the Bible teaches us that believers will not know because we will be raptured. Even if we did know, God would still protect us because scripture tells us that His children are not destined for wrath.

The False Prophet:

The antichrist has a "press secretary" if you will who speaks as the voice of satan. Again we see a mocking of God. The Holy Spirit has a job to speak for Christ. The work of this beast that comes from the earth will speak for satan and allow people to get to know satan and see what a "good guy" he is. This earthly beast is the FALSE PROPHET.

It is interesting that the first beast comes from the sea meaning gentiles. This beast comes from the earth. But that is all it says, we really don't know the culture, race or ethnicity of the false prophet.

Jesus said many false prophets will appear in the last days. The first beast was a political military ruler; this beast will be a religious leader, a false prophet. (See Revelation 16:13, 19:20, 20:10).

End Times in Easy Terms

This religious false prophet has 2 horns like a lamb. Who was described in the Bible as a Lamb? JESUS. Christ had 7 horns (Revelation 5:6) but the false prophet has only 2, indicating less power. Yet he spoke like a dragon. His word will be law and those who defy it will pay with their lives.

Although he coordinates worldwide worship, there really is no indication that he is the head of the one world church.

Satan will infuse the same great authority in the false prophet as he did in the antichrist. By doing this he will again incorporate a worldwide religion. But he goes further than just religion; the false prophet consolidates a worldwide economy and commerce (Revelation 16-17).

This guy will use satanic deception. Great wonders will deceive people to worship the beast and the idol as god. Notice now that we have the dragon, beast and false prophet which is the unholy trinity compared to the Father, Son and Holy Spirit. Another counterfeit that satan puts forth to fool the world.

This false prophet will reorganize the world's population; everyone will have an identifying mark. The Bible says they will receive it on their foreheads or hands.

After a lot of study, I have concluded that other than the number 666 we don't know what it is or how it will be used. It is simply an identifying mark that is able to control the whole world and individual's lives down to what they eat and drink, buy and sell.

End Times in Easy Terms

John closes this sometimes scary part of his vision by saying, "This calls for wisdom." As believers we shouldn't live in panic or fear. Seek wisdom. Perfect love casts out all fear according to 1 John.

We're not called to figure it out; we're called to have wisdom. And though this antichrist has the power of Satan behind him, and will rule through fear and intimidation, his doom is absolute. Our confidence is built on the solid rock of Jesus Christ. The fate of the antichrist is spelled out in Scripture where it says, "And then the lawless one will be revealed, whom the Lord Jesus will overthrow with the breath of his mouth and destroy by the splendor of his coming" (2 Thess.2:8).

This confidence is revealed in the great hymn:

"A Mighty Fortress Is Our God" Did we in our own strength confide, our striving would be losing, were not the right man on our side, the man of God's own choosing. Dost ask who that may be? Christ Jesus, it is he; Lord Sabbaoth his name, from age to age the same and he must win the battle. And though this world, with devils filled, should threaten to undo us, we will not fear, for God hath willed his truth to triumph through us. The Prince of Darkness grim, we tremble not for him; his rage we can endure, for lo, his doom is sure; one little word shall fell him.

Aren't you glad that we can stand on Christ the Solid Rock?

HOW CAN THE ANTI-CHRIST SET HIMESELF UP IN THE TEMPLE IF THERE IS NO TEMPLE IN JERUSALEM NOW?

This is a great question. Many people are wondering if and when a new temple will be built in Jerusalem. At the writing of this book there has been no temple built. In the author's opinion, there will be another temple built sometime before the antichrist sets himself up in it to proclaim himself as god.

Matthew 24:15, "So when you see standing in the holy place 'the abomination that causes desolation,' spoken of through the prophet Daniel—let the reader understand"

2 Thessalonians 2:4, "He will oppose and will exalt himself over everything that is called God or is worshiped, so that he sets himself up in God's temple, proclaiming himself to be God."

Revelation 11:1, "I was given a reed like a measuring rod and was told, "Go and measure the temple of God and the altar, and count the worshipers there."

We see that from the Old Testament to the New Testament there are prophecies that tell us that there will be a temple there in Jerusalem. When it will be built is anyone's guess.

WILL I HAVE TO TAKE THE MARK OF THE BEAST? WHO WILL?

The Bible is very specific about this question so there is not much debate on this topic. The following is a list of verses on the mark of the beast:

Revelation 13:17, "He also forced everyone, small and great, rich and poor, free and slave, to receive a mark on his right hand or on his forehead, so that no one could buy or sell unless he had the mark, which is the name of the beast or the number of his name. This calls for wisdom. If anyone has insight, let him calculate the number of the beast, for it is man's number. His number is 666."

Revelation 14:11, "And the smoke of their torment rises forever and ever. There is no rest day or night for those who worship the beast and his image, or for anyone who receives the mark of his name."

Revelation 16:2, "The first angel went and poured out his bowl on the land, and ugly and painful sores broke out on the people who had the mark of the beast and worshiped his image."

Revelation 19:20, "But the beast was captured, and with him the false prophet who had performed the miraculous signs on his behalf. With these signs he had deluded those who had received the mark of the beast and worshiped his image. The two of them were thrown alive into the fiery lake of burning sulfur."

Do not forget that if you are already a believer the Bible talks about a rapture, believers leaving the earth and meeting Christ in the air. I believe that the people left here after the rapture that go through the tribulation still have a choice. They can choose to worship the One True God- Jehovah or worship the false god. Those who worship the beast will receive the mark. However as we will discover in chapter 8, the message of the tribulation is forgiveness! People will be saved during the tribulation and there will be many who will not choose to take the mark of the beast. Beyond what the scripture plainly tells us is simply guessing and speculation.

WHAT IS THE MARK OF THE BEAST?

This is also in doubt. If we look at the scripture it tells us in Revelation 13:17 that those who take the mark will receive it on their forehead or right hand and the number of the beast is 666.

Does this literally mean a mark on the forehead or right hand or does it mean that the mark is shown by what we do; believing representing the mind or forehead and serving representing the right hand. Thinking and doing, the head and the hand may be symbolized here.

There are many who firmly believe that there will be a literal mark or tattoo of some sort physically on the right hand or forehead. Maybe so but no one knows absolutely for sure.

End Times in Easy Terms

As to what the mark is, again we do not know. Is it the number 666? Is it a symbol? A barcode? A computer chip? Numerous guesses have evolved over the years but the Bible tells us that it will be some identifying mark whether physical or by obedience to the beast that will mark those people as followers of the beast.

WHAT IF PEOPLE REFUSE TO BELIEVE IN GOD. WHAT HAPPENS TO THEM?

The Bible talks about two places; hell and the lake of fire and I believe these are real places the Bible references.

In Matthew 25:41 Jesus tells us that eternal fire was prepared for the devil and his angels. It also seems from that verse that people who refuse to follow Christ will go there. Then in Revelation 20:14 at the end of the judgments it seems that "death" and "hell or hades" will be thrown into the lake of fire and death and hell will be destroyed. Since death and hell or hades are not "people" but places, death and hell are put into the lake of fire or the second death.

Revelation 20:13 says "death and hell gave up the dead that were in them." So after hell gives up the dead, hell is thrown into the lake of fire, however that happens and whatever that means, nobody knows. We just do not know. Then there are the judgments for those who were in hell.

End Times in Easy Terms

In between the time that hell gave up the dead that were in it and hell being thrown into the lake of fire and the judgment of those that were previously in hell, the Bible does not tell us what happens. One might assume from whatever theological interpretation one comes from that all the people from hell would end up in the lake of fire. But it clearly tells us that after the dead were judged, anyone's name that was not found written in the book of life was thrown into the lake of fire.

The Bible says that the devil, beast and false prophet will be tormented in the lake of fire day and night for all eternity.

DO PEOPLE GET A SECOND CHANCE TO BELIEVE IF THEY DID NOT BELIEVE BEFORE THE TRIBULATION STARTED?

This is a great question. There are many who believe very firmly that people do not get a second chance if they refused to believe before the rapture or tribulation. However we do know that many Jews and Gentiles will come to faith in God during the tribulation.

Some use the verse in 2 Thessalonians 2:12 "and so that all will be condemned who have not believed the truth but have delighted in wickedness" to teach that people do not get a second chance. The phrase "have not believed the truth" is taken to mean that people have rejected the truth of Jesus before the rapture or tribulation and therefore they are condemned and cannot be saved.

That verse does not say that people do not have a second chance. It simply says that people who choose not to believe are condemned. There was a time in my life where I did not believe the gospel and did not receive Jesus. In that state of rejection I did not believe the truth. But, through God's love and invitation I decided to receive the mercy and grace that Jesus has to offer and I became a believer in 1974.

In the same way, I believe that in the tribulation, the people refusing to believe in God stand in condemnation. But as the message of the tribulation is forgiveness (Revelation 8) people will heed the call of God and become believers.

Perhaps the short answer is that no one knows in absolute certainty whether people will get a second chance or not. If I were pressed to give an answer I would simply answer with these verses:

Lamentations 3:32, "Though he brings grief, he will show compassion, so great is his unfailing love (mercy)."

Jeremiah 33:11, ""Give thanks to the LORD Almighty, for the LORD is good; his love (mercies) endures forever."

Psalm 136 "His love (mercies) endures forever."

God is just and righteous and gracious and merciful at the same time. It is hard for us to pull this tension together but ultimately we have to leave these answers up to God because we just simply do not know.

The important thing is that you know God through His Son Jesus Christ today! See Appendix A for more information.

WHAT WILL HAPPEN TO AMERICA AND THE OTHER NATIONS OF THE WORLD?

Although the eagle is mentioned in scripture I do not believe that it represents America as some people do. The Bible tells us that there will be nations that partner together to come down to try to defeat Israel. We are told of what seems to be a world made of ten combined nations but again these are in general terms.

I have a book in my library about America in prophecy but I believe the author has made a giant leap of faith in seeing the scriptures as portraying the United States as being mentioned in the Bible. I believe that America will somehow either combine with other countries into a confederated union of some sort or she will have declined economically enough that she is no longer a major player in world events. Perhaps an organization like the United Nations or another controlling force of equal or greater power will be dictating what nations will be doing in the end times. There is always the possibility that something no one has ever thought about will happen. We just do not know for sure. What we do know is that to the very bitter end, we still see Israel in existence and mentioned by name and that tells us that God still has something very important in store for His chosen people.

Study Questions:

1. How would you describe the tribulation? _____
_____

2. What are the reasons for the tribulation? _____
_____
_____

3. What about the Christians and the tribulation? Do you think the Christians or the church will have to go through the tribulation or part of it? Why or why not?
_____
_____
_____
_____

4. Which tribulational view do you hold to and why?
_____
_____
_____
_____

End Times in Easy Terms

5. Who intrigues you the most about the major players in the tribulation? _____

_____

_____

6. What do you think the mark of the beast is? _____

_____

_____

_____

7. Do you think people will get a second chance to believe after the tribulation? Why or why not. Can you give Biblical references for your answer?

_____

_____

_____

_____

_____

End Times in Easy Terms

> *He has delivered us from the domain of darkness and transferred us to the kingdom of his beloved Son, in whom we have redemption, the forgiveness of sins.*
>
> Paul, Colossians 1:13-14

Chapter 8

What is God's Message through the Great Tribulation?

Revelation 15 is the light at the end of the tunnel. All through Revelation we see bowls of wrath, blood, wormwood, visions, death, and through it all God has always been calling for people to repent and turn to Him! What do we see in Revelation that God wants us to know?

End Times in Easy Terms

1. FORGIVENESS: GOD'S MAIN MESSAGE.

When I study Revelation, "Forgiveness" is mentioned 10 times. That is the message of repentance and forgiveness every 2.2 chapters or every 40 verses. Forgiveness is available if you repent.

God is not an eternally angry God delighting in zapping people and making your life miserable. Jesus came to give our lives meaning and to give us an abundant, joyous life!

In Revelation repentance and or forgiveness is mentioned in 3 particular sections; chapters 2-3, 9 and 16. It is interesting that the message of repentance and forgiveness is at the beginning, middle and end of the tribulation. Does that tell you something? It tells me that repentance and forgiveness is continually available to whosoever will call on the name of Jesus during the tribulation.

Why is God sending the plagues, tribulation, earthquakes, and all the disasters on the earth? Revelation 3:19 tells us, "Those whom I love I rebuke and discipline. So be earnest, and repent." Revelation 9:20, "The rest of mankind that were not killed by these plagues still did not repent of the work of their hands." Revelation 16:9, "They were seared by the intense heat and they cursed the name of God, who had control over these plagues, but they refused to repent and glorify him."

Revelation 16:11, "Men gnawed their tongues in agony and cursed the God of heaven because of their pains and their sores, but they refused to repent of what they had done."

See the message? God is sending these things to give people an opportunity to repent. He's showing them how bad it will be if they do not. It doesn't make sense to us, but the tribulation and plagues are a symbol of God's love for mankind to repent!

Forgiveness is God's main message not only throughout the BIBLE but through all of Revelation! Yet John says this is a marvelous sign because with these plagues God's wrath is completed! There is a light at the end of the tunnel! There is a finish to this whole apocalypse of the tribulation. Revelation 15:1.

2. THE PROOF OF FORGIVENESS!

Revelation 15:2-3 we see the tribulation saints! They are people who have turned to God during the tribulation! They have seen the light! They have seen God's love even through the plagues and earthquakes and bitter water and things falling from the sky, they have turned to God and did not worship the beast or take his number into their lives.

They were victorious in the Grace of God! They are proof that all that God is doing in the Tribulation is accomplishing His goal; people repenting and being forgiven and going to heaven.

3. WORSHIPPING BECAUSE OF FORGIVENESS:

These tribulation saints were given harps by God Himself. They sang the songs of Moses and of the Lamb.

What about the Songs of Moses? It was a song written here on earth and they are singing it in heaven! Maybe some of the songs that were written or sung here on earth in honor to God we will be able to sing in heaven! We can see, through this illustration, that some of the songs that were sung here on earth are extended into heaven and with musical instruments! I believe it will be beyond our imagination!

Did you know that the first recorded worship with singing in the Bible is in Exodus when the Israelites were delivered from Egypt and safe after crossing the Red Sea?

Want to hear something amazing? Revelation 15:3 is the last recorded song in the Bible. The theme of the song is about the greatness of God and His deliverance. Isn't it interesting that the first recorded song in Exodus 15 and the last recorded song in Revelation 15 are singing about God's deliverance, forgiveness and grace? AMAZING! And not only that, but in Revelation 15 they were singing THE SONG OF MOSES in Exodus 15! The first and last recorded songs in the Bible were the same song!

They were singing the song of their heart! They were full of praise for God, they were singing His song. Isn't it great when we can get together to sing His Song about His Story!

End Times in Easy Terms

4. THE SYMBOL OF FORGIVENESS IS REVEALED!

Everything Moses built for the Old Testament, the Tabernacle, Ark of the Covenant, all the holy furniture everything he built he did so by seeing the original in Heaven in a vision. The real original heavenly tabernacle and Ark of the Covenant is in heaven still and here we see it opened up and revealed in Revelation 15:5.

When we ask the question, "what did the Ark of the Covenant do or symbolize here on earth" it shows us what it does in heaven.

On earth:

(1) God's presence dwelt between the angels on the top of the Ark of the Covenant.

(2) It housed the 10 commandments (2nd ed.), Aaron's rod and a jar of manna.

(3) Once a year the blood from the sacrificial lamb was sprinkled on the top of the Ark and that represented that the people's sins had been forgiven. The Ark's focus was forgiveness.

In Revelation 15 in the middle of the chapter the Ark of the Covenant is revealed showing the symbol of sacrifice, deliverance and forgiveness! What a story, what a message, over and over repentance and forgiveness all through the tribulation!

5. THE OPPORTUNITY FOR FORGIVENESS IS GIVEN:

In Revelation 15:6-8, I find it strange that out of the tabernacle and temple, the symbol of forgiveness, comes the last seven angels with seven plagues. Isn't that strange?

But WHY does God send the plagues in the first place? He does this to get people to repent and receive forgiveness. It is funny how God works in mysterious ways.

No one could enter the temple in heaven until the seven plagues were completed. No matter what it looks like to us, The Smoke (God's Glory) is always manifested during times of Judgment and Forgiveness. The judgments and opportunity for repentance was a holy time and the temple was off limits because God was doing His redemptive work of inviting people to repent and receive forgiveness.

Let me tell you my story of forgiveness that I'll never forget. This story isn't the biggest story in the world, not the most dramatic but to a 10 year old little boy it was pretty meaningful. An orange hunting vest is my symbol of forgiveness.

Deer hunting is a big deal in Arkansas, where I grew up. It's a family tradition passed down through generations. When I was about 10 my grandpa took me hunting that year and I wanted to borrow my dad's lucky hunting vest. It was great, it had dried deer blood on it, snags from briers, and I knew I could get a deer if I wore that vest.

End Times in Easy Terms

I asked dad and he said, "Well I don't know . . . don't lose it, that's my favorite vest." I promised. I got his vest we went hunting and I didn't get a deer. But when we got back to the jeep, I took it off and put it on the spare tire. And there it stayed, and we pulled off and when we got home it was lost somewhere along the miles.

There was a light at the end of the tunnel, but I knew it was a train! Judgment is coming. My light wasn't deliverance. I knew I had to tell him, so I took a deep breath, manned up; I did the manly thing. . . I called him from my grandpa's house!

I explained what happened and kept saying I'm sorry, I'm sorry. And after my explanation there was a long pause (here it comes) and he said, "That's ok. It's just a vest." "But I lost your lucky hunting vest" I said. "That's ok, don't worry about it. It's just a vest."

Now that may not seem like a lot to you but that was the world to me at the time. I'm a middle aged man now and I still get choked up over the story because it showed the forgiveness that we're supposed to have and that God has for us.

In Revelation 15, the forgiven were singing the songs of deliverance and forgiveness. What is your song? What is the preoccupation of your life; the theme of your worship? How are you expressing that to God?

Some are singing the songs of redemption! Some are singing the blues. It is a tough world. We live in a negative world. The economy is tanking, unemployment is rising, money is tight, the average American family is up to their eyeballs in debt, we work all week, we're tired and we don't see an end.

If you've had a tough week and you're feeling beat up by relationships, work, and the realities of life, I want you to be encouraged. Jesus wants to lead you into a fuller worship experience. He wants you to see Him as your all in all. There is a light at the end of the tunnel and it is God's grace, deliverance, forgiveness and love.

Study Questions:

1. What is God's main message throughout the Great Tribulation? _____

2. What book and chapter is the main message of the tribulation taught? _____

End Times in Easy Terms

3. What group of people do we see in Revelation 15:2-3?
_____

4. What is significant about the song in Exodus and the song in Revelation?
_____
_____
_____

5. What does the Ark of the Covenant point to?
_____
_____
_____

6. Why does God allow so much pain and suffering in the tribulation?
_____
_____
_____

7. Have you truly been forgiven by God?
_____
_____
_____
_____

> I saw an Angel descending out of Heaven. He carried the key to the Abyss and a chain—a huge chain. He grabbed the Dragon, that old Snake—the very Devil, Satan himself!—chained him up for a thousand years.
>
> Revelation 20:1-2

Chapter 9

The Millennium

The Millennium is known as "The Thousand Year Reign of Christ." Just like the word "rapture" is never mentioned in the Bible, the word "millennium" is also never mentioned but Revelation references it by calling it "One thousand years" in Revelation 20:2-6, "He seized the dragon, that ancient serpent, who is the devil, or Satan, and bound him for a thousand years. He threw him into the Abyss, and locked and sealed it over him, to keep him from deceiving the nations anymore until the thousand years were ended. After that, he must be set free for a short time. I saw thrones on which were seated those who had been given authority to judge. And I saw the souls of those who had been beheaded because of their testimony for Jesus and because of the word of God. They had not worshiped the beast or his image and had not received his mark on their foreheads or their hands. They came to life and reigned with Christ a thousand years. (The rest of the dead did not come to life until the thousand years were ended.) This is the first resurrection. Blessed and holy are those who have part in the first resurrection. The second death has no power over them, but they will be priests of God and of Christ and will reign with him for a thousand years."

As with any end time event, there are always many guesses, interpretations and valid theological viewpoints as to what they mean and the millennium is no exception. I believe the thousand year reign with Christ is a literal one thousand years and it has a definite purpose.

At this point I will mention the three major millennial views with a very short definition. As with any view there are different variations of these points.

1. Pre-Millennial View: This view teaches that Jesus Christ will PHYSICALLY return and set foot on the earth just prior to establishing His millennial or 1000 year reign. I personally hold to this interpretation. This is the viewpoint from which this book has been written.

2. Post-Millennial View: This view teaches that Christ's return to earth will be after the millennium, which is described as a golden age on earth in which Christian ethics prosper.

3. Amillennialism: When there is an "a" in front of a word it usually means or denotes "no", As in "no millennium." This view teaches that there will be no physical 1000 year reign of Christ on the earth. It views the phrase in Revelation 20 as a symbolic number, not literal, for a very long time.

WHAT IS THE REASON FOR THE THOUSAND YEAR REIGN WITH CHRIST?

It fulfills the covenant made with Abraham to give Israel all the land that God had promised them and that they would live in peace in the land.

Genesis 15:18-21 "On that day the LORD made a covenant with Abram and said, "To your descendants I give this land, from the rivers of Egypt to the great river, the Euphrates— the land of the Kenites, Kenizzites, Kadmonites, Hittites, Perizzites, Rephaites, Amorites, Canaanites, Girgashites and Jebusites."

These are other references to the covenant that will be fulfilled to Israel during the Millennial Reign; Gen.12:7; 13:15, 17; 15:7-8, 18; 17:8; 24:7; 26:3; 28:13-14; 35:12; 48:4; 50:24.

The fulfillments go deeper than what is mentioned here. If this interests you I again suggest you find a study book or commentary that describes the covenants of God.

End Times in Easy Terms

WHAT WILL THE MILLENNIAL REIGN BE LIKE?

- It will be here on earth.

Revelation 5:10 and 20:6 make it clear that the reign will be on the earth.

- It will be in Jerusalem.

Isaiah 2:2-3 "In the last days the mountain of the LORD's temple will be established as chief among the mountains; it will be raised above the hills, and all nations will stream to it. Many peoples will come and say, "Come, let us go up to the mountain of the LORD, to the house of the God of Jacob. He will teach us his ways, so that we may walk in his paths." The law will go out from Zion, the word of the LORD from Jerusalem."

It also references this in chapters 6-12 in Zechariah which talk about the temple in Jerusalem after Christ's return. Zechariah 8:20-23 says, "This is what the LORD Almighty says: "Many peoples and the inhabitants of many cities will yet come, and the inhabitants of one city will go to another and say, 'Let us go at once to entreat the LORD and seek the LORD Almighty. I myself am going.' And many peoples and powerful nations will come to Jerusalem to seek the LORD Almighty and to entreat him." This is what the LORD Almighty says: "In those days ten men from all languages and nations will take firm hold of one Jew by the hem of his robe and say, 'Let us go with you, because we have heard that God is with you.'"

End Times in Easy Terms

- It will be a time of total peace on earth.

"Nation shall not lift up sword against nation, neither shall they learn war anymore." Isaiah 2:4.

Satan will be cast into the bottomless pit to fall for one thousand years, Revelation 20:1-3 "And I saw an angel coming down out of heaven, having the key to the Abyss and holding in his hand a great chain. He seized the dragon, that ancient serpent, who is the devil, or Satan, and bound him for a thousand years. He threw him into the Abyss, and locked and sealed it over him, to keep him from deceiving the nations anymore until the thousand years were ended. After that, he must be set free for a short time."

- There will be an absence of sin or its influences on earth during the millennial reign.

Micah 4:1-5 "In the last days the mountain of the LORD's temple will be established as chief among the mountains; it will be raised above the hills, and peoples will stream to it. Many nations will come and say, "Come, let us go up to the mountain of the LORD, to the house of the God of Jacob. He will teach us his ways, so that we may walk in his paths." The law will go out from Zion, the word of the LORD from Jerusalem. He will judge between many peoples and will settle disputes for strong nations far and wide. They will beat their swords into plowshares and their spears into pruning hooks.

Nation will not take up sword against nation, nor will they train for war anymore.

Every man will sit under his own vine and under his own fig tree, and no one will make them afraid, for the LORD Almighty has spoken. All the nations may walk in the name of their gods; we will walk in the name of the LORD our God forever and ever."

- It will be a time of peace even among the animal world

Isaiah 11:6-9 "The wolf will live with the lamb, the leopard will lie down with the goat, the calf and the lion and the yearling together; and a little child will lead them. The cow will feed with the bear, their young will lie down together, and the lion will eat straw like the ox. The infant will play near the hole of the cobra, and the young child put his hand into the viper's nest. They will neither harm nor destroy on all my holy mountain, for the earth will be full of the knowledge of the LORD as the waters cover the sea."

- It seems as if people will live much longer

Isaiah 65:19-23 "I will rejoice over Jerusalem and take delight in my people; the sound of weeping and of crying will be heard in it no more. "Never again will there be in it an infant who lives but a few days, or an old man who does not live out his years; he who dies at a hundred will be thought a mere youth; he who fails to reach a hundred will be considered accursed. They will build houses and dwell in them; they will plant vineyards and eat their fruit. No longer will they build houses and others live in them, or plant and others eat. For as the days of a tree, so will be the days of my people; my chosen ones will long enjoy the works of their hands. They will not toil in vain or bear children doomed to misfortune; for they will be a people blessed by the LORD, they and their descendants with them.

WHAT HAPPENS AFTER THE ONE THOUSAND YEARS ARE OVER?

As we saw in Revelation 20:3 satan will be let loose for a short time after being in the abyss or bottomless pit for 1000 years during which time the peaceful Millennial Reign of Christ is happening on earth.

Most premillennial interpretations believe that after the 1000 years is over and satan is loosed, satan will gather nations to come and fight against Israel one last time to try to destroy her.

The media uses "Armageddon" in many ways to denote a great catastrophic or cataclysmic event that brings wide destruction, but the book of Revelation uses the word only once.

Revelation 16:12-16 describes the Battle of Armageddon where all the nations try to destroy Israel and Jerusalem in particular, "The sixth angel poured out his bowl on the great river Euphrates, and its water was dried up to prepare the way for the kings from the East. Then I saw three evil spirits that looked like frogs; they came out of the mouth of the dragon, out of the mouth of the beast and out of the mouth of the false prophet. They are spirits of demons performing miraculous signs, and they go out to the kings of the whole world, to gather them for the battle on the great day of God Almighty. "Behold, I come like a thief! Blessed is he who stays awake and keeps his clothes with him, so that he may not go naked and be shamefully exposed." Then they gathered the kings together to the place that in Hebrew is called Armageddon."

This battle is also mentioned in the Old Testament but it is not called "Armageddon." Look at a few of these verses:

Zechariah 14:2-4 "I will gather all the nations to Jerusalem to fight against it; the city will be captured, the houses ransacked, and the women raped. Half of the city will go into exile, but the rest of the people will not be taken from the city. Then the LORD will go out and fight against those nations, as he fights in the day of battle. On that day his feet will stand on the Mount of Olives, east of Jerusalem, and the Mount of Olives will be split in two from east to west, forming a great valley, with half of the mountain moving north and half moving south."

Zechariah 14:12-16 "This is the plague with which the LORD will strike all the nations that fought against Jerusalem: Their flesh will rot while they are still standing on their feet, their eyes will rot in their sockets, and their tongues will rot in their mouths. On that day men will be stricken by the LORD with great panic. Each man will seize the hand of another, and they will

End Times in Easy Terms

attack each other. Judah too will fight at Jerusalem. The wealth of all the surrounding nations will be collected—great quantities of gold and silver and clothing. A similar plague will strike the horses and mules, the camels and donkeys, and all the animals in those camps.

Then the survivors from all the nations that have attacked Jerusalem will go up year after year to worship the King, the LORD Almighty, and to celebrate the Feast of Tabernacles."

So from these verses and viewpoint of interpretation it looks like there is the great and final battle of Armageddon where the world's nations try to defeat Israel. But as seen in these verses, God will defeat all the nations and God will be victorious! Revelation 20:7-10 tells us about that victory, "When the thousand years are over, Satan will be released from his prison and will go out to deceive the nations in the four corners of the earth—Gog and Magog—to gather them for battle. In number they are like the sand on the seashore. They marched across the breadth of the earth and surrounded the camp of God's people, the city he loves. But fire came down from heaven and devoured them. And the devil, who deceived them, was thrown into the lake of burning sulfur, where the beast and the false prophet had been thrown. They will be tormented day and night forever and ever."

After Christ is victorious, then comes the final Judgment and the New Heaven and New Earth! AMEN!

End Times in Easy Terms

Study Questions:

1. Which Millennial view sounds more "biblical" in your opinion? WHY?

_____

_____

_____

2. Of all the characteristics of the Millennial Reign, what sounds the best to you and what was the most surprising thing that you discovered?

_____

_____

_____

3. Why is there a 1000 year reign anyway? (Assuming one believes in it?)

_____

_____

_____

_____

End Times in Easy Terms

4. In your opinion why is satan thrown into the abyss or bottomless pit for 1000 years. Do you think he is "falling" for 1000 years or could it mean something else?

_____

_____

_____

_____

_____

5. Why do you think God let satan out of the abyss to try to fight against Him and Israel for one last time? Why didn't God just leave satan in the abyss?

_____

_____

_____

6. What is the greatest thing about the great last battle of Armageddon?

_____

_____

_____

_____

_____

> "Heaven would be a very hell to a wicked person."
> — David Berg

Chapter 10

What Will Heaven Be Like?

In the year 125 AD, a Greek named Aristides wrote to a friend about Christianity explaining why this "new religion" was so successful; "If any righteous man from among the Christians passes from this world, they rejoice and offer thanks to God, and they escort his body with songs and thanksgiving as if he were setting out from one place to another nearby." That's so true isn't it? We are heading to another place and that is called heaven. We have a wonderful description of heaven here in Revelation 21.

Let's ask some basic questions about heaven.

End Times in Easy Terms

1. What is Heaven?

Heaven is referred to over 500 times in the Bible and 60 times just in Revelation. It is God's dwelling place. 1 Kings 8:27, "The highest heaven cannot contain You!" Psalm 33:14, "from his dwelling place he watches all who live on earth" Even Jesus taught us to pray, "Our Father who art in heaven."

2. Where is Heaven?

From an earthly perspective Heaven is UP! No matter where you are on the planet! Jesus said in John 6:41, "I am the Bread of life that came down from heaven." When Jesus ascended to heaven, He was taken UP.

3. What will Heaven be like?

- Totally New: Revelation 21:1-2, "Then I saw a new heaven and a new earth. The first heaven and the first earth disappeared. And I saw the Holy City, the new Jerusalem, coming down out of heaven from God, prepared and ready."

Really the only physical description we have of heaven is in the capital city called the New Jerusalem. This is actually a fulfillment of an Old Testament prophecy found in Isaiah 65:17, "The Lord says, "I am making a new earth and new heavens." This is an interesting concept, the word NEW here means new in

KIND not in time. It will be a totally new earth in "form or quality that has never existed before."

- Has a Capital City: Revelation 21:2, "I saw the Holy City, the new Jerusalem, coming down out of heaven from God, prepared as a bride beautifully dressed for her husband."

The New Jerusalem is not heaven but it comes down out of heaven and is like the Capital City of Heaven. Heaven is called Heaven in scripture but the New Jerusalem is called the City.

- Has Enough Room for Everyone: In Revelation 21 we have a very detailed description of the "the City" in verses 15 and 16.

This City or the New Jerusalem is 1400 miles wide, 1400 miles deep and 1400 miles high. It is a perfect cube.

Let's have fun speculating for a moment. This 1400 mile cube could have 100's of floors and each floor has 1,960,000 square miles on each floor (1400 times 1400). If each floor in the New Jerusalem is ONE mile high between floors that means there would be 1400 floors. And each floor has almost 2 million square miles. 1400 floors would have 2 trillion 744 billion square miles.

If the floors were 1/2 mile apart there would be 2800 floors meaning 5 Trillion 488 Billion square miles. Did you know that the total square miles of ALL the land on earth is only about 57 million square miles? And the New Jerusalem could easily have almost 6 TRILLION Square miles. That's the equivalent to 30 earths if the earth were a solid land mass with no water! Could you imagine if the floors were a spacious 12 feet between there would be over 600,000 floors TIMES almost 2 million square miles each! I'll let you do the math on that one.

Just one floor of the New Jerusalem is a little over 1/2 the size of the U.S. In 2012 the global population was estimated at approaching 7 billion. Given the size of the New Jerusalem, easily over 250 BILLION people could live there. It is estimated that less than 10 billion people have ever lived from the beginning of time to today. Just the capital city alone (not counting heaven) could hold over 100's of billions of people.

I suggest that there will be plenty of room for you to play whatever you want in the Capital city and there will be plenty of room for everyone to live in as much space as they want. That's incredible!

- Place of Eternal Happiness: Revelation 21:4, "He will wipe away all tears from their eyes. There will be no more death, no more grief or crying or pain. The old things have disappeared."

Did you know tears, death, pain, sorrow are all the results of sin and sinful bodies. In heaven there will be none of that.

Not only will we be perfect but we will be in eternal happiness! Revelation just told us old things are passed away.

End Times in Easy Terms

Isaiah 65:17b, "the former things will not be remembered, nor will they come to mind." And verse 18 "Be glad and rejoice forever in what I create. The New Jerusalem I make will be full of joy, and her people will be happy."

- A Place of Dazzling Beauty:

I encourage you to take a moment now and read Revelation 21:17-27! Just the walls of the City are about 216 feet thick! On a football field that would be 72 yards thick. Look at all the beautiful colors and decorations and precious stones! The streets are made of gold so pure and shiny that it looked like transparent glass. In the economy we live in today everyone tells us to invest in gold. In heaven we will walk on streets of gold and travel through the huge gates made of a single pearl each!

Think about this. What causes a pearl to be formed in an oyster? An irritant like a grain of sand gets into the oyster and a substance called nacre is formed over it to protect the oyster and a pearl is created. The gates made of pearl are a reminder to us that access into the city is made possible only by the suffering of our Savior on the Cross to pay the ultimate price for our admission.

We're told that God is the Temple, God is the Light and the Gates never close because access to the New Jerusalem is always open.

Think about this, if God is not limited in any area, and His mind is infinite then Heaven will be the most wonderful place the Mind of God can conceive and the Hand of God can create! Words do not have the power to describe that kind of place.

That's why 1 Corinthians 2:9 says "No eye has seen, no ear has heard, no mind has conceived what God has prepared for those who love him" and yet verse 10 is hardly ever read after that, "And yet God has revealed it to us by His Spirit." God has given us insights into what heaven will be like.

- A Place of Purity:

Maybe the most attractive thing about heaven is found in Revelation 21:27, "But nothing that is impure will enter the city, nor anyone who does shameful things or tells lies. Only those whose names are written in the Lamb's book of the living will enter the city."

As it is described in the Bible, the New Jerusalem seems to hover between heaven and earth and it has gates for us to enter in and out of to go to Heaven, New Jerusalem and New Earth. Can you imagine traveling at the speed of thought? Just think and you're there. I could think and be somewhere as far away as another country just as fast as I could think and be in the closest town next to me. I believe we will be able to travel at the speed of thought as we navigate our way through heaven.

We could go on and on about what kind of place heaven will be like. There are good books on the market just about heaven. If you are further intrigued I encourage you to give one of those a try.

Study Questions:

1. What is heaven?

_____
_____

2. Where is heaven in your opinion?

_____
_____
_____

3. What are your thoughts on how big the New Jerusalem will be?

_____
_____
_____
_____

4. Can you list at least 4 wonderful characteristics of heaven?

_____
_____
_____

5. Why do you think the gate of Pearl is significant?

_____

_____

_____

_____

_____

6. What do you personally think will be the greatest thing about heaven? Why?

_____

_____

_____

_____

_____

_____

End Times in Easy Terms

> We are going to spend eternity in another world. ... Is it not natural that we should look and listen and try to find out who is already there and what is the route to take?
>
> Dwight L. Moody

Chapter 11

What happens after the end of Revelation?

The simple answer is "more than our minds can even comprehend!" The Bible tells us in Revelation that on the new earth there seems be governments and leaders, Revelation 21:24 and nations Revelation 21:26, 22:2. We have already discussed that there will be all languages, tribes, and ethnicities in heaven. We will still be who God created us to be.

The Bible seems to tell us that we will be active, worshipping, singing, serving, and who knows whatever else! God created in me a desire and talent to carve and paint. I just wonder if that is what God gave me here, will I get to carve and

End Times in Easy Terms

paint to God's glory in heaven? We do not know but the thoughts are just mind boggling!

There is a vast universe or many universes "out there" that man will never see here on this earth that God created all for His glory. Perhaps through eternity we will get to discover all the creations of God. Maybe we will be able to travel through the universe or look at the stars or nebulae, or galaxies! Whatever we will be able to do, I believe in awestruck wonder we will give God glory for things He has saved just for us when we get to heaven!

Truly, we do not know what awaits us but whatever it will be, it will be the best and greatest that the mind of God could create and for me, that is enough.

Study Questions:

1. What is the coolest or most surprising thing you learned from this study?

_____
_____
_____
_____
_____

End Times in Easy Terms

2. After this study are you more excited about the end times, more scared, more confused, more confident or a combination of two of these?

_____

_____

_____

_____

_____

_____

_____

3. Why do you think God left a lot of these end times topics so vague? Why didn't He clarify them more? Why is Revelation so confusing?

_____

_____

_____

_____

4. Would you be confident to try to explain some of these topics to your friends or family who asks you now that you have finished this study? Why or why not?

_____

_____

_____

_____

> *Sometimes the questions are complicated and the answers are simple."*
> Dr. Seuss

Chapter 12

KIDS ASK:

Q: When Jesus comes back, are the Christians going to rise through the ceiling or will they just disappear and leave their clothes behind?

A: The Bible doesn't say anything about what will happen to our clothes. But we do know a little bit of what will happen according to Matthew 24:36-41. We will be living out life as normal. Jesus tells about that day when He comes back. Jesus says, "That is how it will be at the coming of the Son of Man. Two men will be in the field; one will be taken and the other left. Two women will be grinding with a hand mill; one will be taken and the other left."

End Times in Easy Terms

When the Bible tells us that we will be "caught up" it means "seized" or "taken up." So perhaps if we are in a building when it happens, we will go up through the ceiling, but it happens so fast that it seems as if we just disappear. It happens so fast that we probably will not realize we're rising through the ceiling. When Jesus comes back, all of a sudden we will just be with Him in the air, if we are Christians. 1 Corinthians 15:51-52.

Q: Does the Christian's actual body come out of the grave?

A: Yes, but it will be a perfect body without defects, diseases and whole. 1 Corinthians 15:51-53.

Q: Can the spirits who come with Jesus or the people standing around see the bodies coming out of the ground?

A: Again, the Bible tells us that this whole event of the rapture will happen so fast that those with Jesus or those standing around at the time may not be able to see it happen.
1 Corinthians 15:52

Q: When Jesus comes and people disappear, will the nonbelievers who are left think aliens took them or something?

A: The Bible doesn't tell us what the people will think or how they will explain it away. Perhaps they will say that aliens abducted a bunch of people. It may be explained away by some

End Times in Easy Terms

scientific method. There will certainly be some who will have heard that the rapture will happen but did not accept Jesus into their heart and were left behind. It would probably be true to say that many people will know exactly what happened.

Q: Will the people who are left behind be scared and call the police?

A: I am sure that many people will be scared because their friends and loved ones will be missing. The police will probably be called but they will not be able to do anything about it.

Q: Will my pets be in heaven?

A: The Bible does not say anything about our pets going to heaven but I believe there will be animals in heaven or on the new earth that God recreated. Just as the Garden of Eden was pure and full of animals as God's creation, I believe heaven will be full of animals as well. There are not any verses that talk about this but if the Garden of Eden was a picture of heaven, I believe there will be animals there.

Q: Will there be plants in heaven?

A: Yes, the Bible talks about a Tree of Life and its leaves, about a river and I believe that there will be many plants in heaven and on the new earth that God recreated. I believe it will be like God originally intended for it to be in the Garden of Eden. Revelation 22:1-2

Q: Will I have to wear glasses in heaven?

A: No. Our bodies will be perfect and we will have no need for anything like that. YEA! 1 Corinthians 15:51-52

Q: Why does God want the world to end?

A: There is a big plan to bring the world to a place to where He can recreate the earth. Just like we can be born again and become a new creature, the earth will be "born again" in a sense and God will make a new earth. In order for that to happen God must bring everything that is going on to a conclusion. The way He does that is up to Him and shown to us in the book of Revelation. Revelation 21:1

Q: How did satan sin against God?

A: He was prideful and wanted to ascend above the throne of God and he wanted to become God. One third of the angels in heaven sided with satan but God overthrew them and cast them to earth. I believe we have a picture of satan's pride and fall in Isaiah 14:12-15 and in Ezekiel 28:11-19.

End Times in Easy Terms

> *"Life is the art of drawing sufficient conclusions from insufficient premises."*
> — Samuel Butler

Chapter 13

CONCLUSION

Whether you found yourself agreeing or disagreeing with some of my conclusions or interpretations, it is not my intention to try to get you to believe the scriptures the way I have presented them. My goal is to draw our attention to the fact that Jesus is coming again in some way and in some manner. This is the big picture.

As believers we have the privilege to be living in the Kingdom; loving God, loving others and living the life God calls us to live. There is a great freedom in not having to have everything figured out. There is freedom in not quite understanding the tension that we see in the scriptures concerning the end times.

End Times in Easy Terms

Personally, I am glad God did not put me on the agenda committee for the last days and end times. I am guessing you are not on that committee either. Perhaps, when we all get to heaven we might look at each other when it is all over and say, "We were all wrong!"

I strongly believe we are not "saved" to sit and wait for Jesus to come back. I believe we are "saved" to serve the Kingdom. We are exhorted all throughout the scripture to live lives worthy of the calling of God.

It is my prayer that because of the fact that Jesus is coming back one day that you will be ready and live a worthy life as we live out the Kingdom in these last days.

APPENDIX A:

HOW TO BE READY

If Jesus were to return today would you be ready? It may be that you have picked this book up out of curiosity. You would like to know what the Bible has to say about the end times. But you don't feel ready if the Lord Jesus should come at THIS moment.

What do you need to do to be ready to go to heaven with Jesus? I like to describe it as simple as A-B-C-D.

<u>A: Admit.</u> You must ADMIT that you are a sinner and have done some things wrong in your life. The Bible says in Romans 3:23, "For all have sinned, and come short of the glory of God." The word *sin* means to "miss the mark." We've fallen short of perfection. 1 John 1:8 says, "If we say that we have no sin, we deceive ourselves, and the truth is not in us." We all have sin so we must admit that to God."

<u>B: Believe.</u> You must BELIEVE in the Lord Jesus Christ and what He did for you through His life, death, burial and

End Times in Easy Terms

resurrection from the dead." Romans 10:9 tells us that if we believe in our heart that God has raised Jesus from the dead, we will be saved. We don't have to understand it. We simply must believe it, because without faith it is impossible to please God, Hebrews 11:6.

C: Confess and Call. We must CONFESS our sins to God. The word "confess" means "to agree with." We must agree with God that we are sinners.

1 John 1:9 tells us that if we do confess our sins to God He will forgive us! CALL on Jesus to save you from your sins. Acts 2:21 tells us that whoever will CALL on the name of Jesus will be saved. We call on Jesus through praying to Him.

D: Decide. Everyone must decide for themselves. This decision is not something anyone, even a priest or a preacher can do for you. It is a personal decision on your part to ask Jesus to forgive you of your sins, to come into your life and save you. You are asking Jesus to be the boss and director of your life!

When that happens we have the promise in 2 Corinthians 5:17 that we will become a NEW creation! The old things will pass away and all things will become new in our life. What a wonderful promise!

If that is something you would like for your life, you can say a simple prayer something like this in your heart and sincerely mean it to the Lord:

End Times in Easy Terms

Dear Jesus, I know I am a sinner. I am asking You today to forgive me of all my sins. Make me a new person from the inside out. I am asking You to come into my life and save me. I ask You to be the Boss and Director of my life from this time forward. Thank You Jesus for saving me. As a new believer help me live for You. AMEN.

Remember "a" prayer won't save you; it's the attitude of your heart. But if you just prayed that prayer in sincerity to God then, CONGRATULATIONS! You are now a child of God and a new believer in Christ. As a believer, you now stand assured that when the coming or the rapture of Jesus happens, you will be prepared in your heart to go. You now have eternal life and you don't have to fear that you will be left behind! 1 John 5:13.

APPENDIX B

DATE SETTERS THROUGH THE AGES

I want to thank Todd Strandberg for giving me permission to use this list of date setters throughout history from his website; http://www.raptureready.com/rr-date-setters.html

53 AD

Even before all the books of the Bible were written, there was talk that Christ's return had already taken place. The Thessalonians panicked on Paul when they heard a rumor that the day of the Lord was at hand, and they had missed the rapture.

500

A Roman priest living in the second century predicted Christ would return in 500 AD, based on the dimensions of Noah's ark.

End Times in Easy Terms

1000

This year goes down as one of the most heightened periods of hysteria over the return of Christ. All members of society seemed affected by the prediction that Jesus was coming back at the start of the new millennium. None of the events required by the Bible were transpiring at that time; the magic of the number 1000 was the sole reason for the expectation. During concluding months of 999 AD, everyone was on his best behavior; worldly goods were sold and given to the poor; swarms of pilgrims headed east to meet the Lord at Jerusalem; buildings went unrepaired; crops were left unplanted; and criminals were set free from jails. When the year 999 AD turned into 1000 AD, nothing happened.

1033

This year was cited as the beginning of the millennium because it marked 1,000 years since Christ's crucifixion.

1186

The "Letter of Toledo" warned everyone to hide in the caves and mountains. The world was reportedly to be destroyed with only a few spared.

1420

The Taborites of Czechoslovakia predicted every city would be annihilated by fire. Only five mountain strongholds would be saved.

1524-1526

Muntzer, a leader of German peasants, announced that the return

End Times in Easy Terms

of Christ was near. After Muntzer and his men destroyed the high and mighty, the Lord would supposedly return. This belief led to an uneven battle against government troops. He was strategically outnumbered. Muntzer claimed to have had a vision from God in which the Lord promised that He would catch the cannonballs of the enemy in the sleeves of His cloak. The prediction within the vision turned out to be false when Muntzer and his followers were mowed down by cannon fire.

1534

A repeat of the Muntzer affair occurred a few years later. This time, Jan Matthewhys took over the city of Munster. The city was to be the only one spared from destruction. The inhabitants of Munster chased out by Matthewhys and his men, regrouped and lay siege to the city. Within a year, everyone in the city was dead.

1650-1660

The Fifth Monarchy Men looked for Jesus to establish a theocracy. They took up arms and tried to seize England by force. The movement died when the British monarchy was restored in 1660.

1666

For the citizens of London, 1666 was not a banner year. A bubonic plague outbreak killed 100,000 and the Great Fire of London struck the same year. The world seemed at an end to most Londoners. The fact that the year ended with the Beast's number—666--didn't help matters.

End Times in Easy Terms

1809

Mary Bateman, who specialized in fortune telling, had a magic chicken that laid eggs with end-time messages on them. One message said that Christ was coming. The uproar she created ended when an unannounced visitor caught her forcing an egg into the hen's oviduct. Mary later was hanged for poisoning a wealthy client. History does not record whether the offended chicken attended the hanging.

1814

Spiritualist Joanna Southcott made the startling claim that she, by virgin birth, would produce the second Jesus Christ. Her abdomen began to swell and so did the crowds of people around her. The time for the birth came and passed; she died soon after. An autopsy revealed she had experienced a false pregnancy.

1836

John Wesley wrote that "the time, times and half a time" of Revelation 12:14 were the years between 1058-1836, "when Christ should come" (A. M. Morris, The Prophecies Unveiled, p. 361).

1843-1844

William Miller was the founder of an end-times movement that was so prominent it received its own name, Millerism. From his studies of the Bible, Miller determined that the second coming would happen sometime between 1843-1844. A spectacular meteor shower in 1833 gave the movement a good push forward.

End Times in Easy Terms

The buildup of anticipation continued until March 21, 1844, when Miller's one-year timetable ran out. Some followers set another date--Oct 22, 1844. This too failed, collapsing the movement. One follower described the days after the failed predictions: "The world made merry over the old Prophet's predicament. The taunts and jeers of the 'scoffers' were well-nigh unbearable."

1859

Revelationist Thomas Parker, a Massachusetts minister, looked for the millennium to start about 1859.

1881

Someone who was called "Mother Shipton" had, 400 years earlier, claimed that the world would end in 1881. A controversy hangs over the Shipton writings as to whether or not publishers doctored the text. If the date was wrong, should it matter anyway?

1910

The revealing of Halley's Comet was, for many, an indication of the Lord's second coming. The earth actually passed through the gaseous tail of the comet. One enterprising man sold comet pills to people for protection against the effects of the toxic gases.

1914

Charles Russell, after being exposed to the teachings of William Miller, founded his own organization that evolved into the Jehovah's Witnesses. In 1914, Russell predicted the return of Jesus Christ.

End Times in Easy Terms

1918

In 1918, new math didn't help the Witnesses from striking out again.

1925

The Witnesses had no better luck in 1925. They already possessed the title of "Most Wrong Predictions." They would expand upon it in the years to come.

1941

Once again, Jehovah's Witnesses believed that Armageddon was due. Before the end of 1941, the end of all things was predicted.

1967

When the city of Jerusalem was reclaimed by the Jews in 1967, prophecy watchers declared that the "Time of the Gentiles" had come to an end.

1970

The True Light Church of Christ made its claim to fame by incorrectly forecasting the return of Jesus. A number of church members had quit their livelihoods ahead of the promised advent.

1973

A comet that turned out to be a visual disappointment nonetheless compelled one preacher to announce that it would be a sign of the Lord's return.

1975

The Jehovah's Witnesses were back at it in 1975. The failure of the forecast did not affect the growth of the movement. The

End Times in Easy Terms

Watchtower magazine, a major Witness periodical, has over 13 million subscribers.

1977

We all remember the killer bee scare of the late 1970's. One prophecy prognosticator linked the bees to Revelation 9:3-12. After 20 years of progression, the bees are still in Texas. I'm beginning to think of them as the killer snails.

1981

One author boldly declared that the rapture would occur before December 31, 1981, based on Christian prophecy, astronomy, and a dash of ecological fatalism. He pegged the date to Jesus' promised return to earth a generation after Israel's rebirth. He also made references to the "Jupiter Effect," a planetary alignment occurring every 179 years that supposedly could lead to earthquakes and nuclear plant meltdowns.

1982

It was all going to end in 1982, when the planets lined up and created magnetic forces that would bring Armageddon to the earth.

1982

A group called the Tara Centers placed full-page advertisements in many major newspapers for the weekend of April 24-25, 1982, announcing: "The Christ is Now Here!" They predicted that He was to make himself known "within the next two months." After the date passed, they said that the delay was only because the

End Times in Easy Terms

"consciousness of the human race was not quite right..." Boy, all these years and we're still not ready.

1984

The Jehovah's Witnesses made sure, in 1984, that no one else would be able to top their record of most wrong doomsday predictions. The Witnesses' record currently holds at nine. The years are: 1874, 1878, 1881, 1910, 1914, 1918, 1925, 1975, and 1984. Lately, the JWs are claiming they're out of the prediction business, but it's hard to teach old dog new tricks. They'll be back.

1987

The Harmonic Convergence was planned for August 16-17, 1987, and several New Age events were also to occur at that time. The second coming of the serpent god of peace and the Hopi dance awakening were two examples.

1988

The book, *88 Reasons Why the Rapture is in 1988,* came out only a few months before the event was to take place. What little time the book had, it used effectively. By the time the predicted dates, September 11-13, rolled around, whole churches were caught up in the excitement the book generated. In the dorm where we lived, my friends were also openly confronting all of the unsaved. I found it necessary to help defuse certain situations.

In one case, an accosted "sinner" was contemplating disciplinary action against one of those trying to convert him. Finally, the dates of destiny dawned and then set. No Jesus had come. The environment was not the same as Miller's 1844 failure. To my surprise, the taunting by the unsaved was very brief. I made one other interesting observation. Although the time for the rapture had been predicted to fall within a three-day window, September 11-13, my friends gave up hope on the morning of the 12th. I pointed out that they still had two days left, but they had already begun to lose hope.

1989

After the passing of the deadline in *88 Reasons*, the author, Edgar Whisenant, came out with a new book called *89 Reasons Why the Rapture is in 1989*. This book sold only a fraction of the number of copies his prior release had sold.

1991

A group in Australia predicted Jesus would return through the Sydney Harbor at 9 a.m., March 31, 1991.

1991

Nation of Islam leader Louis Farrakhan proclaimed the Gulf War would be "the War of Armageddon ... the final War."

1991

Menachem Schneerson, a Russian-born rabbi, called for the Messiah to come by September 9, 1991, the start of the Jewish New Year.

1992

A Korean group called Mission for the Coming Days had the Korean Church an uproar in the fall of 1992. They foresaw

End Times in Easy Terms

October 28, 1992 as the date for the rapture. Numerology was the basis for the date. Several camera shots that left ghostly images on pictures were thought to be a supernatural confirmation of the date.

1993

If the year 2000 is the end of the 6,000-year cycle, then the rapture must take place in 1993, because you would need seven years of the tribulation. This was the thinking of a number of prophecy writers.

1994

In the book, *1994: The Year of Destiny*, F. M. Riley foretold of God's plan to rapture His people. The name of his ministry is "The Last Call," and he operates out of Missouri.

1994

Pastor John Hinkle of Christ Church in Los Angeles caused quite a stir when he announced he had received a vision from God that warned of apocalyptic event on June 9, 1994. Hinkle, quoting God, said, "On Thursday June the 9th, I will rip the evil out of this world." At the time, I knew Hinkle's vision didn't match up with Scripture. From a proper reading of Bible prophecy, the only thing that God could possibly rip from the earth would be the Christian Church, and I don't think God would refer to the Church as "evil." Some people tried to interpret Hinkle's unscriptural vision to mean that God would the rip evil out of our hearts when

End Times in Easy Terms

He raptured us. Well, the date came and went with no heart surgery or rapture.

1994

Harold Camping, in his book *Are You Ready?*, predicted the Lord would return in September 1994. The book was full of numerology that added up to 1994 as the date of Christ's return.

1994

After promising they would not make anymore end time predictions, the Jehovah's Witnesses fell off the wagon and proclaimed 1994 as the conclusion of an 80-year generation; the year 1914 was the starting point.

1996

This year had a special month, according to one author who foresaw September as the time for our Lord's return. The Church Age will last 2,000 years from the time of Christ's birth in 4 BC.

1996

California psychic Sheldon Nidle predicted the end would come with the convergence of 16 million space ships and a host of angels upon the earth on December 17, 1996. Nidle explained the passing of the date by claiming the angels placed us in a holographic projection to preserve us and give us a second chance.

1997

In regard to 1997, I received several e-mail messages that pointed to this as the year when Jesus would return for His church. Two of the more widely known time frames were Monte Judah's prediction that the tribulation would begin in February/March and another prediction based on numerology and the Psalms that targeted May 14 as the date of the rapture.

1997

When Yitzhak Rabin and Yasser Arafat signed their peace pact on the White House lawn on September 13, 1993, some saw the events as the beginning of tribulation. With the signing of the peace agreement, Daniel's 1,260-day countdown was underway. By adding 1,260 days to September 1993, you arrive at February 24, 1997.

1997

Stan Johnson of the Prophecy Club saw a "90 percent" chance that the tribulation would start September 12, 1997. He based his conclusion on several end-time signs: that would be Jesus' 2,000th birthday and it would also be the Day of Atonement, although it wouldn't be what is currently the Jewish Day of Atonement. Further supporting evidence came from Romanian pastor Dumitru Duduman. In several heavenly visions, Dumitru claimed to have seen the Book of Life. In one of his earlier visions, there were several pages yet to be completed. In his last vision, he noticed the Book of Life only had one page left. Doing some rough calculating, Johnson and friends figured the latest time frame for the completion of the book would have to be September 1997.

End Times in Easy Terms

1998

Numerology: Because 666 times three equals 1998, some people point to this year as being prophetically significant.

1998

A Taiwanese cult operating out of Garland, Texas predicted Christ would return on March 31 of 1998. The group's leader, Heng-ming Chen, announced God would return and then invite the cult members aboard a UFO.

The group abandoned their prediction when a precursor event failed to take place. The cult's leader had said that God would appear on every channel 18 of every TV in the world.

1998

On April 30, 1998, Israel was to turn 50 and many believed this birthday would mark the beginning of the tribulation. The reasoning behind this date has to do with God's age requirement for the priesthood, which is between 30-50.

1998

1998 Marilyn Agee, in her book, *The End of the Age*, had her sights set on May 31, 1998. This date was to conclude the 6,000-year cycle from the time of Adam. Agee looked for the rapture to take place on Pentecost, which is also known as "the Feast of Weeks." Another indicator of this date was the fact that the Holy Spirit did not descend upon the apostles until 50 days after Christ's resurrection. Israel was born in 1948; add the 50 days as years and you come up with 1998.

End Times in Easy Terms

After her May 31 rapture date failed, Agee, unable to face up to her error, continued her date setting by using various Scripture references to point to June 7, 14, 21 and about 10 other dates.

1999

Well, you can't call Marilyn Agee a quitter. After bombing out badly several time in 1998, Marilyn set a new date for the rapture: May 21 or 22 of this year.

1999

TV newscaster-turned-psychic Charles Criswell King had said in 1968 that the world as we know it would cease to exist on August 18, 1999.

1999

Philip Berg, a rabbi at the Kabbalah Learning Center in New York, proclaimed that the end might arrive on September 11, 1999, when "a ball of fire will descend . . . destroying almost all of mankind, all vegetation, all forms of life."

2000

Numerology: If you divide 2,000 by 3, you will get the devil's number: 666.66666666666667.

2000

The names of the people and organizations that called for the return of Christ at the turn of the century is too long to be listed here.

End Times in Easy Terms

2000

On May 5, 2000, all of the planets were supposed to have been in alignment. This was said to cause the earth to suffer earthquakes, volcanic eruption, and various other nasty stuff. A similar alignment occurred in 1982 and nothing happened. People failed to realize that the other nine planets only exert a very tiny gravitational pull on the earth. If you were to add up the gravitational force from the rest of the planets, the total would only amount to a fraction of the tug the moon has on the earth.

2000

According to Michael Rood, the end times have a prophetically complicated connection to Israel's spring barley harvest. The Day of the Lord began on May 5, 2000. Rood's fall feast calendar called for the Russian Gog-Magog invasion of Israel to take place at sundown on October 28, 2000.

2000-2001

Dr. Dale SumburËru looked for March 22, 1997 to be "the date when all the dramatic events leading through the tribulation to the return of Christ should begin" The actual date of Christ's return could be somewhere between July 2000 and March 2001. Dr. SumburËru is more general about the timing of Christ's second coming than most writers. He states, "The day the Lord returns is currently unknown because He said [Jesus] these days are cut short and it is not yet clear by how much and in what manner they

End Times in Easy Terms

are cut short. If the above assumptions are not correct, my margin of error would be in weeks, or perhaps months."

2002

Priests from Cuba's Afro-Caribbean Yoruba religion predicted a dramatic year of tragedy and crisis for the world in 2002, ranging from coups and war to disease and flooding.

2004

This date for Jesus' return is based upon psalmology, numerology, the biblical 360 days per year, Jewish holidays, and "biblical astronomy." To figure out this date, you'll need a calculator, a slide rule, and plenty of scratch paper.

2011-2018

For the past several decades, Jack Van Impe has hinted at nearly every year as being the time for the rapture. Normally, he has only gone out one or two years from the current calendar year. However, Jack's latest projection for the rapture goes out several years. His new math uses 51 years as the length of a generation. If you add 51 years to 1967, the year Israel recaptured Jerusalem, you get 2018. Once you subtract the seven-year tribulation period, you arrive at 2011.

2012

New Age writers cite Mayan and Aztec calendars that predict the end of the age on December 21, 2012.

2060

Sir Isaac Newton, Britain's greatest scientist spent 50 years and

End Times in Easy Terms

wrote 4,500 pages trying to predict when the end of the world was coming. The most definitive date he set for the apocalypse, which he scribbled on a scrap of paper, was 2060.

An untold number of people have tried to predict the Lord's return by using elaborate timetables. Most date setters do not realize that mankind has not kept an unwavering record of time. Anyone wanting to chart, for example, 100 BC to 2000 AD, would have to contend with the fact that 46 BC was 445 days long, there was no year 0 BC, and in 1582 we switched from Julian Years (360 days) to Gregorian (365 days). Because most prognosticators are not aware of all of these errors, their math is immediately off by several years.

Made in the USA
Charleston, SC
16 October 2013